*We are all storytellers, ~~...~~
That's what we do. That~~...~~
power as human beings.*
—RICHARD WAGAMESE

*There is no life that does not
contribute to history.*
—DOROTHY WEST

To Mark Leslie Taylor and Bonnie Sheppard,
who love museums and whose help and
support were unflagging.

We would like to acknowledge that when we visit,
work or research in the museums in this book
we are working and exploring on the traditional
and unceded territories of the following First Nations
people:

ʔaqʼam
Dakelh
Ktunaxa
Lhtako Dené
Nlakaʼpamux
Secwepemc
Sinixt
syilx/Okanagan
syilx/Sqilxw
Tsilhqotʼin
Upper Similkameen
Westbank
Yaqan Nukiy (Lower Kootenay)

WE RECOGNIZE THAT THESE MANY FIRST NATIONS HAVE THOUSANDS
OF YEARS OF CULTURE AND HISTORY ON THIS LAND, CULTURE AND
HISTORY WE VALUE AND HOPE TO LEARN FROM.

TABLE OF CONTENTS

WHAT IS A MUSEUM?

What is a museum? Can it have galleries outside? Can it be housed in a strip mall? A jail? On a boat? In an airport or hotel?

Is it still a museum if it's small? Or does it have to be grand? Do museums only belong in fancy cities or can a small town have one too? What do you think?

What makes something worth keeping in a museum? Does it have to cost a lot of money? Be exceptionally old? Incredibly rare? Do the belongings in a museum have to stay there all the time? Or can they take a holiday?

How does something end up in a museum? Can it be donated by someone's mom? Your best friend? My dad, Dave? Or your teacher? Is there something you have you think belongs in a museum? (And don't say your scary next-door neighbour!)

The world's oldest museum was built by a Babylonian princess 2,500 years ago. Today, in Canada, there are over 2,300 museums. That means you could visit a museum a day for over six years. What are you waiting for? Get visiting. Just imagine all those stories waiting to be heard.

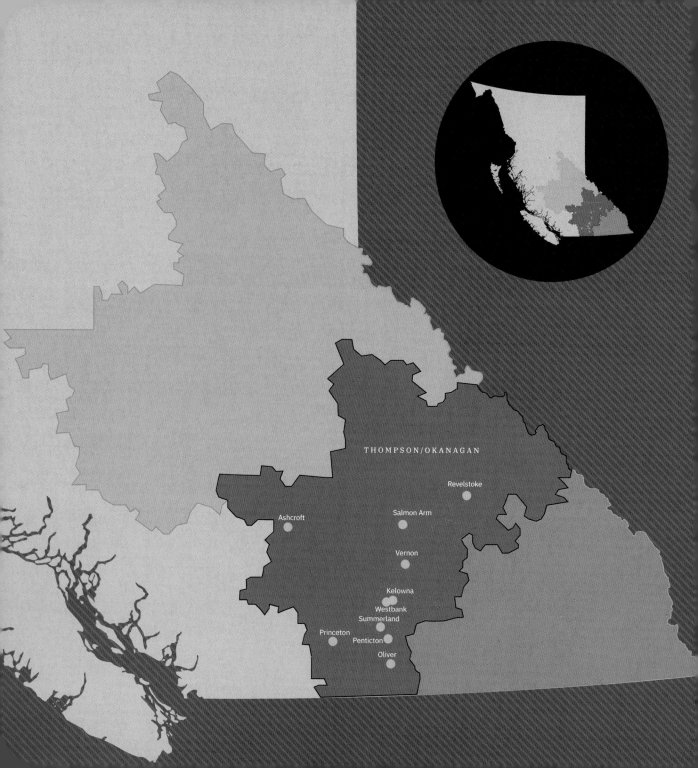

THOMPSON/OKANAGAN

Revelstoke

Ashcroft

Salmon Arm

Vernon

Kelowna

Westbank

Summerland

Princeton

Penticton

Oliver

THOMPSON/ OKANAGAN

TRADITIONAL AND UNCEDED TERRITORY OF THE FOLLOWING FIRST NATIONS:

Ktunaxa

Nlaka'pamux

Secwepemc

Sinixt

syilx/Sqilxw

syilx/Okanagan

Upper Similkameen

Westbank

1

ASHCROFT MUSEUM

the old post office
building c. 1900
Photo: Ashcroft Museum

The old post office building today

Ashcroft

THOMPSON RIVER

Brink st.

Railway Ave.

4th st.

→ **Museum**

Barnes rd.

JUST THE FACTS

WHERE IS IT? 404 Brink St., Ashcroft, BC, V0K 1A0;
(250) 453-9232
ashcroftbc.ca/museum

ARE PHOTOGRAPHS ALLOWED? Please ask staff regarding photos.

HOW DID IT START? R. D. Cumming lived in the Ashcroft area from the 1880s. In 1912, he bought *The Journal*, the local newspaper. Cumming loved writing, history and photography. He also loved collecting things. He collected so many items he set them up in the loft above the newspaper office so other people could see them. He opened the first Ashcroft museum in 1935 in that same space.

WHERE HAS IT LIVED?

The loft space above *The Journal* office became too small, so the museum moved to the Harvey Bailey Warehouse, which was owned by the Canadian Pacific Railway (CPR). That was in the early 1950s. When Canadian Pacific wanted to tear its building down, the Cumming family donated the items in their collection to the town. This was a wonderful gift, but there was nowhere to put the collection. The items were put in storage while a new building was constructed.

Finally, in 1958, the town opened a new building that contained both the museum and the fire hall. Museum objects have to be treated very carefully and this building was not the best place to keep objects in good condition. In 1982, the museum moved to the old post office building (which had also housed the **customs office**, telegraph office and telephone exchange). Before the museum moved in, the building was remodelled so the collection would be conserved properly.

WHERE DO THE ITEMS COME FROM?

The museum collects objects that have a local connection and help visitors understand the history of the area. Many people want to give items to the museum, but because there is limited space for displays and storage, it accepts only things it doesn't already have.

HOW HAS IT CHANGED?

Many items from the Cumming collection are still displayed in the museum. But today you can also find objects that show the history of the local First Nations people and highlight the contribution the Chinese community made to Ashcroft.

In a museum you can:

Learn about how technology has changed

TELEPHONE EXCHANGE

The Switchboard

The Cranktelephone

If you wanted to make a call, you turned a crank on the side of the phone.

Telephones were connected by kilometers of copper wire stretched between telephone poles.

In the early 20th century, all telephones were attached to wires coming into homes or offices.

A switchboard operator connected you to the person you were trying to call.

All around the world, switchboard operators connected people who wanted to talk to each other.

Switchboard operators were mostly women and were called "Hello Girls".

A voice answered, *"Hello. Number please."*

You couldn't pick up the phone and call a friend, family member, or the doctor directly.

A telephone switchboard operator from 1915
Photo: Kelowna Public Archives: KPA#131

JUST THE FACTS

HORSE FLY NET

WHAT IS IT? The horse fly net is a woven net that was put over a horse's back to keep the flies off.

WHAT DOES IT LOOK LIKE? The net was made with leather and a thin, lightweight nylon material that was constructed in a webbing and cord fashion. It had a fringe that moved when the horse did, scaring the flies away.

WHERE DOES IT COME FROM? The Haddocks were the first family to move to Ashcroft in 1886. Their house still stands on Brink Street. Thelma Haddock was the granddaughter of this first family. When Thelma died in 1976, her companion Alma Loyst of Walhachin, BC, donated the fly net to the museum. This fly net is one of over 200 artifacts of Thelma's that have been donated.

WHO USED IT? Thelma Haddock used this fly net to protect her horses from flies, bugs and birds. The net also protected them from the elements when they were outdoors.

Tell Me More

Would you like to own a racehorse? In the 1940s, Thelma Haddock owned two racehorses that were considered the finest in the interior of British Columbia. On July 1, 1944, she returned home with four prizes won by her horses Teri Grinus and Lady Diskin at the Quesnel Races and Celebration. Thelma frequently put fly nets on her horses before and after a race.

The Haddock family, c. 1900
Source: Ashcroft Museum

? WOULD YOU BELIEVE?

There are approximately 250 wild horses that roam the Highland Valley area, about 40 kilometres from Ashcroft. These horses escaped nearby ranches and farms forming wild herds. In the spring, summer and fall the horses eat grass, but in the winter, when the snow is covering the grass, the workers at the Highland Valley Copper Mine feed the horses. These horses will never know what it's like to wear a horse net or a horse blanket.

My Turn

What could you use to weave a blanket? Are there plants in your neighbourhood that could be used?

CONNECTIONS

Thelma Haddock treated her horses very well. But before the gas motor was invented, horses worked very hard pulling trolleys, brewery wagons, carriages and delivery carts. Some of these horses were treated very badly. The humane societies in many northern states in the USA were determined to change that.

They wanted a law that said if a workhorse was standing still (not working), it must be covered by a blanket. They believed blankets would protect horses from getting chills. If drivers did not obey the law, they were fined or sent to jail.

The idea of making the horses' lives better was a good one, but horses were often left with wet or badly worn blankets that didn't improve their lives. Blankets were often shared among horses and carried diseases.

★ WHY IS THE HORSE FLY NET IMPORTANT IN THIS AREA?

In its **heyday**, Ashcroft was the supply station for towns in northern British Columbia. The town was filled with horses and oxen pulling freight wagons and the famous BX stagecoaches, all heading to or coming back from as far away as Fort George. Horses were the main form of transportation in those days.

Horses were also a great source of entertainment. Ashcroft's main street, Railway Avenue, was straight and a perfect length for the one-mile dash. Crowds of people would line up along the sidelines of the racing strip to watch and cheer on their favourite horses.

Of course, with the presence of lots of manure from the workhorses, the oxen and the racehorses, there would have been lots of flies and thus the importance of the fly net.

Ashcroft Street scene, undated
Source: prairie-towns.com

JUST THE FACTS

TOMATO KNIFE

WHAT IS IT? This was a tool used by the workers in the canning factory to core and peel tomatoes.

WHAT DOES IT LOOK LIKE? The knife is 14 centimetres in length, with a wooden handle and a curved metal blade that looks more like a pointy spoon than a knife blade.

WHERE DOES IT COME FROM? The tomato knife came from the Ashcroft Cannery when it shut down in 1957. Ken Schubert donated it in 2000.

WHO USED IT? After the tomatoes were steamed, cannery workers used the tomato knife to prepare tomatoes for canning.

The Ashcroft Cannery
Photo: Ashcroft Museum

Tell Me More

Would waking up at 6 a.m., starting work at 7 a.m. and working until 7:00 at night be worth missing the first ten days of school in September? The Ashcroft Cannery (1924 – 1957) employed men, women and high school students. For many students, working at the cannery was a great job. They missed the first ten days of school during the peak canning time then worked part-time after school to make some spending money.

Ashcroft Cannery employees did many kinds of jobs like sorting, steaming, coring and peeling tomatoes, and supervising the production and quality of goods being produced. Women peelers using a knife just like this one were paid on a piecework basis of five cents for every pan of peeled tomatoes. The pans held just over 13 litres of peeled tomatoes, or about the same amount as 16 large cans of store-bought tomatoes. The average peeler earned about $3.50 per day. Can you figure out how many pans a peeler would have to fill to make $3.50? Some expert peelers made as much as $5.00 per day. How many pans would they have to fill?

8

⭐ WHY IS THE TOMATO KNIFE IMPORTANT IN THIS AREA?

Who would have expected a small knife like this to save a town from poverty? In the early 1900s, it was hard to get a job in Ashcroft. The Great Fire of 1916 destroyed most of the downtown businesses. Stable workers, harness and carriage makers and blacksmiths were in less demand because the BC Express stagecoach company shut down. Trains and motor vehicles had taken over from horses. Many people turned to farming. Chinese farmers were experts at irrigation because they had learned this skill growing up in China. They grew and sold large, juicy tomatoes. What they didn't sell locally, they shipped by rail to other parts of British Columbia.

When the manager of the BC Express Company saw railcars filled with tomatoes leaving town, he wondered why Ashcroft could not process its own tomatoes. He turned his company's freight barn into a cannery. Farmers and merchants, many of them Chinese, supplied the cannery. Because of the cannery, there were many jobs for local people and people from outside Ashcroft. Every year, during harvest, farmers hired pickers. The cannery employed hundreds of inside workers and truck drivers.

For 33 years, the Ashcroft Cannery produced tomato juice, canned tomatoes and ketchup. But by 1957 the United States was selling vegetables to Canada at such low prices, the cannery had too much competition and was forced to shut down.

My Turn

With supervision from an adult, try to peel a tomato. Is it easier to peel if the tomato is put in boiling water for one minute?

CONNECTIONS

The Aztecs were one of the first cultures to farm tomatoes and include them in their cooking. We have no idea whether or not the Aztecs used a knife like this to peel tomatoes. In the 1500s, Hernan Cortez, a Spanish **conquistador,** conquered the Aztecs and claimed Mexico for Spain. He may have been the first man to bring the tomato to Europe.

FERNANDO CORTES

Photo: Wikimedia Commons, Daderot

CANNERY WORKERS WANTED

Starting Early in August, we will require about forty girls to peel and sort Tomatoes in our Cannery at Ashcroft, B.C.

Applications received now. Write for Particulars.

Ashcroft Canners Ltd. - - - - - Ashcroft. B. C.

Top: Want Ad for workers,
Bottom: Cannery staff
Photos: Ashcroft Museum

R. J. HANEY HERITAGE VILLAGE & MUSEUM

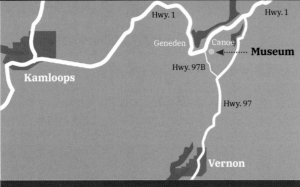

Hwy. 1

Geneden   Canoe

Hwy. 1

Museum

Hwy. 97B

Kamloops

Hwy. 97

Vernon

JUST THE FACTS

WHERE IS IT? 751 BC-97B, Salmon Arm, BC, V1E 4P7;
(250) 832-5243
salmonarmmuseum.org

ARE PHOTOGRAPHS ALLOWED? Yes.

HOW DID IT START? When R. J. Haney's daughter, Marjorie Fulton, passed away in 1984, she left her family's home and 16 hectares of property to the District of Salmon Arm. The one condition was that the Salmon Arm Museum and Heritage Association manage the facility as a public park in memory of her father.

WHERE HAS IT LIVED?

In 1984, the Museum and Heritage Association carried out Marjorie Fulton's wishes. What has changed is what is in the park. It has become a village. The one building that has been on the property from the beginning is R. J. and Margaret Haney's house, built around 1910. Some of the buildings, like the Mount Ida church, Broadview School, and Queest lookout tower, were moved onto the property. The Chinese cookhouse and the filling station were taken apart and put back together on the site. Other buildings, like the blacksmith shop and the fire hall, are reproductions – they were built to look like the originals.

WHERE DO THE ITEMS COME FROM?

Objects are donated or loaned to the Salmon Arm Museum.

HOW HAS IT CHANGED?

The most recent change is the addition of the 1115 square metre Montebello Building. It is now home to the archives, offices, a gallery and a gift store. Also newly constructed are the nine **dioramas** that show what businesses would have looked like in the early 1900s. Just like today, there were places to bank, buy groceries, mail a letter, get your hair cut, buy a newspaper and even get a new hat.

In a museum you can:

learn about one tool settlers' children used in school.

A SCHOOL SLATE

The old schoolhouse at Salmon Arm.
Photo: Archives at R.J. Haney Heritage Village and Museum

In the 1800s and early 1900s paper was too expensive for children to use in school, so they did their schoolwork on a slate.

It's about the size of a tablet and about as thick as your finger.

Slate is sedimentary rock that splits easily into thin slabs.

This slate was used by a boy named Arthur, who wrote his name on the frame.

A slate is like a mini chalkboard with a wooden frame.

Students used a damp rag to clean their slates .

Slates were very delicate and scratched easily so students had to be very careful with them.

Teachers checked and corrected students' work on their slates.

JUST THE FACTS

WHAT IS IT? As the name suggests, this is a bucket used for throwing water on fires to put them out.

WHAT DOES IT LOOK LIKE? The fire bucket is about the same size as a pail you would use in your home for washing the car. It has a round bottom and a handle attached to the bottom.

WHERE DOES IT COME FROM? The bucket is on permanent loan from the Salmon Arm Volunteer Fire Department. That means the bucket will stay at the museum, but the museum does not own it.

WHO USED IT? In small rural communities, firefighters were (and still are) often volunteers. They were friends and neighbours who came together to battle fires in the town and surrounding areas. If there were a fire, an alarm would call the firefighters to the station. Early on in Salmon Arm, the alarm was a large triangle hanging on a telephone pole. Later, the town bought a siren.

These buckets were used in 1909 at a time when all firefighters were men.

Tell Me More

When there was a fire, the firefighters would form a human chain between where they got their water and the fire. They would pass the buckets from person to person. The last person in the line would throw water on the fire. The empty buckets would then be passed back down a second line to the water source.

› R. J. HANEY HERITAGE VILLAGE & MUSEUM

FIRE BUCKET

The bottom of this fire bucket is round. It can't stand up on its own. Don't you think it's weird having a bucket that would fall over if someone wasn't holding it? The fire buckets had rounded bottoms so people wouldn't borrow them and use them for other purposes. The specially made bottoms meant the buckets stayed in the fire hall.

The handle on the base of the bucket was also very useful when throwing water at a fire.

CONNECTIONS

Salmon Arm was lucky not to have a fire brigade led by Marcus Licinius Crassus. He lived in ancient Rome and he created the first Roman fire brigade. He wasn't very nice. If your building was on fire, he offered to buy it from you for very little money. If you agreed, he and his brigade put out the fire. But if you didn't, he left, letting your building burn to the ground.

You can see some fire buckets on the wagon in this old photo

Photo: Archives at R.J. Haney Heritage Village and Museum

My Turn

It is estimated that the bucket brigade used about 570,000 litres of water to put out the 1929 fire. If you were trying to explain how much that was to a much younger person, what would you compare that volume to?

WHY IS THE FIRE BUCKET IMPORTANT IN THIS AREA?

Fires are always dangerous, especially when buildings are made of wood and stand very close to each other.

Today, if modern buildings are connected, they have firewalls between them to help stop or slow down the spread of fire. But in Salmon Arm in February 1929, there were no firewalls. A gasoline lamp in the Regent Café on Front Street burst. Fire raced through the roof of the kitchen and spread to neighbouring businesses. Volunteer firefighters were not the only ones to join the bucket brigade. Clarence Nelson, a long time Salmon Arm resident, helped put out the fire. "When the fire [alarm] went, I wanted to help. I hitched up the team [of horses] to the sleigh and rode the two miles into town," says Nelson. "We just wanted to save what we could for somebody."

The volunteers couldn't save everything, but if the bucket brigade hadn't worked so hard, the whole downtown would have been burnt to the ground. This fire, the largest Salmon Arm had ever seen, cost local businesses close to half a million dollars in today's money.

JUST THE FACTS

WHAT IS IT? The Amberola reproducer is a very early record player.

WHAT DOES IT LOOK LIKE? The player is about the size of a legal-sized filing drawer or a cardboard banker's box. If it sat on your desk at school, it would take up most of the surface area.

WHERE DOES IT COME FROM? The reproducer belonged to a private collector name Sam Beemish. He loved antique record players and used them to play really old recordings from as far back as the 1890s. He had a radio show called Cobweb Corners from 1956 to 1976. It started in Kamloops but later it was also broadcast in the Okanagan and the Cariboo. He played lots of old music on his show.

Sam Beemish donated his collection of cylinders, records and players to the museum. He said it was the largest collection in western Canada.

WHO USED IT? In the early 1900s, music players were not portable. You couldn't listen to music on your phone or tablet. There were no streaming services or playlists. If a family owned an Amberola reproducer, children were probably not allowed to touch it. This record player cost $65 in 1913, which is about $1,700 today. Listening to music played on the reproducer would have been a whole family activity. Back then, however, children would have listened to what their parents were listening to.

> R. J. HANEY HERITAGE VILLAGE & MUSEUM

AMBEROLA REPRODUCER RECORD PLAYER

WOULD YOU BELIEVE?

Think about how portable our music is today. This record player was considered compact. The speaker (or horn) was built into the player. Compared to earlier models that had large horns attached to them, this record player was easy to move and took up much less space. It could even sit on a table.

Tell Me More

Turntables or record players have once again become popular. Before records were flat, however, they looked like a round tube. Sounds were imprinted on the plastic-like, tubular record. These cylinders could be changed, just like records can be changed on a turntable. To play music, you placed a cylinder onto the mandrel, a rod that held the cylinder, and locked it on so it didn't slip off. Then you used a crank to wind up the machine. When you released a little brake, a needle moved along the grooves on the cylinder and you could hear your favourite tunes. Compared to today, the sound was scratchy.

This record player was available in Canada in 1913 from the Eaton's catalogue. Large department stores delivered catalogues to houses in their areas or sent them to people in small towns. These catalogues showed all the things people could buy in that store. The reproducer had to be shipped to Salmon Arm by train. There was one song on each cylinder or record lasting four minutes. Each cylinder or record cost 65 cents.

My Turn

Record your voice on a recording device. When you play it back, does your voice sound the same as you imagined? If it sounds different than you expected, why do you think that is?

CONNECTIONS

Of course, today, modern reproducers are used all over the world. In the last 100 years, we have reproduced voices and other sounds on records made from vinyl and tapes made from plastic tape with a magnetic coating. We have reproduced sound on compact discs and now, digitally, on our computers, tablets and phones.

⭐ WHY IS THE REPRODUCER IMPORTANT IN THIS AREA?

When this player was sold, Salmon Arm did not have a radio or television station. The only other way to hear music was live. You either went to a concert or made music yourself.

With the invention of the reproducer, families could hear their favourite music in their own homes.

Family with an Amberola cylinder phonograph, 1920

3

HISTORIC O'KEEFE RANCH

Photo: Historic O'Keefe Ranch

JUST THE FACTS

WHERE IS IT? 9380 BC-97, Vernon, BC, V1H 1W9; (250) 542-7868
okeeferanch.ca

ARE PHOTOGRAPHS ALLOWED? Yes.

HOW DID IT START? In 1867, Cornelius O'Keefe pre-empted approximately 65 hectares of land at the north end of Okanagan Lake. That's about 160 soccer pitches. "Pre-empting" means he received the land free from the government, which said European settlers could settle on land that did not have anyone living on it.

The syilx/Okanagan people, whose territory covered 69,000 square kilometres, including the area around the north end of the lake, were semi-nomadic. They had permanent homes in the winter but in the summer created temporary homes where they hunted and fished.

Because the syilx/Okanagan people were not living permanently (that is, they didn't have any permanent structures) on the land O'Keefe wanted, he was given the land by the government. Over the next 40 years, he bought more land from the government and from other ranchers, eventually owning 4800 hectares.

He sold off most of his property in 1907. He and his wife kept a small part of the ranch. One hundred years after O'Keefe bought the original property, his son and daughter-in-law turned the ranch into a heritage site. They opened it to the public in 1967.

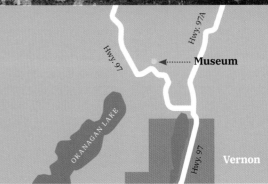

WHERE HAS IT LIVED?

The ranch has been in its current location since 1867. The blacksmith shop was located across the street, but when the O'Keefe family decided to open the ranch as a heritage site, they built a **replica** blacksmith shop where you see it today. The family also reconstructed the general store, which had been the first post office in the Okanagan.

WHERE DO THE ITEMS COME FROM?

Most of the items were donated by the O'Keefe family, but some have been donated by local residents.

HOW HAS IT CHANGED?

After ten years of operating the ranch, the O'Keefe family sold the land, buildings and artifacts to a foundation that gave the ranch to the City of Vernon. It is run by the O'Keefe Ranch and Interior Heritage Society, which oversees the care of the ranch's 10,000 artifacts, as well as thousands of archival documents and photographs.

discover unusual facts about paintings.

PAINTING OF AN ENGLISH GENTLEMAN

Artists use **perspective**, light and shadow when they paint to make the subject look three-dimensional, not flat.

This framed painting is as wide as your bedroom door and as tall as your kitchen counter.

You may change where you are standing, but the perspective light and shadow used by the artist does not change.

Before she had her six children, Elizabeth O'Keefe loved to paint.

When you move around the room, the man's eyes follow you.

Later, Elizabeth O'Keefe bought this painting to display in her home.

If the sitter is looking straight out of the painting, their eyes will appear to follow you.

If the sitter is looking sideways, the eyes will not follow you.

Painting by LM Kilpin

JUST THE FACTS

WHAT IS IT? A butter churn was used to turn cream into butter before there were machines to do it.

WHAT DOES IT LOOK LIKE? The main part of the butter churn is barrel-shaped. It sits on a metal stand that holds it off the ground. The barrel can rock back and forth.

WHERE DOES IT COME FROM? This rocking butter churn originally came from London, Ontario, in around 1900. It was made by the Wortman and Ward company. The O'Keefe family may not have used this churn. Before they opened the ranch as a historic site, they collected many antiques. This may have been one of them.

WHO USED IT? Mostly women would have used this churn, but both boys and girls were often put to work churning butter for the family.

⭐ WHY IS THE BUTTER CHURN IMPORTANT IN THIS AREA?

In rural areas in the 1800s, butter churns were common household items. Only wealthy families in larger towns could afford to buy butter – everyone else had to make it. Sometimes, if farmers had extra butter, they would sell it to shops in town. This butter churn helps us understand how people lived before electricity.

› HISTORIC O'KEEFE RANCH

BUTTER CHURN

We have many modern household appliances with which we could make butter, but we are so used to going to the grocery store and buying butter we never even think of it.

Margarine is often confused with butter. It is an oil product, not a dairy product, and it was once banned in Canada. Because of a federal law, Canadians could not make or import margarine from 1886 to 1917 and from 1922 until 1949.

Tell Me More

Making butter required planning, patience and muscle. Milk straight from the cow had to sit at least 24 hours in a cool place to allow cream to rise to the top. You can't make butter without cream, so homemakers would have to be sure to plan ahead.

Once the cream was skimmed off, the person making the butter would pour the cream into the barrel and start to rock it back and forth. This butter churn had two ways of rocking: using the foot pedal or the handle. Which do you think would have been easier?

It would take almost an hour for the cream to become butter, and there weren't any video games or television shows to help the butter churner pass the time.

Raw Milk → Cream → CHURNING → Skim Milk

My Turn

You can make your own butter with an adult's help. You need heavy cream (the higher the fat content, the better) and a small Mason jar with a lid that screws down tightly. Fill the Mason jar halfway with the cream. Put on the lid. Now start shaking. Shake as hard as you can, so the cream smashes against the lid and the bottom of the jar. After two minutes open the jar. It should look like whipped cream. But that's not butter. Replace the lid and keep shaking. Shake as hard as you can for another six minutes. Open the jar again. The solids and the liquids should be separated. If not, keep shaking. If so, you can pour off the liquid into a bowl. That liquid is buttermilk. It can be used to make pancakes and other delicious breads and desserts. The solid that is left is butter.

CONNECTIONS

In Africa and the Near East, ancient cultures made butter by filling a goatskin bag halfway with cream, blowing air into the bag and then sealing it. The skin was hung on tent poles or a tripod made of sticks and rocked until butter was formed.

Photo: A. Forder

The world's earliest butters were made from the milk of **yak**, sheep and goats. That's because cows weren't yet farm animals.

JUST THE FACTS

WHAT IS IT? It is a round mirror set inside a frame.

WHAT DOES IT LOOK LIKE? This mirror sits inside a wide wooden frame inset with large animal horns. The mirror is not huge, about 40 centimetres in diameter, but all the animal horns make it quite thick.

WHERE DOES IT COME FROM? The mirror came from Liverpool in England.

WHO USED IT? The mother of the house used the mirror.

MRS. O'KEEFE'S BABYSITTING MIRROR

Tell Me More

With today's technology, parents can keep an eye on their children with tiny cameras. But in the 1800s and early 1900s, Mrs. Elizabeth O'Keefe discovered a different way to make sure her children were behaving. This mirror was mounted in a very special place on the wall, so that when Mrs. O'Keefe was entertaining guests in the parlour (a room like our modern-day living room) she could see upstairs. She would know if any of her children sneaked out of bed to play when they were supposed to be sleeping.

Today's technology makes it possible to make cameras really small.

My Turn

With help from an adult, look on the internet and find a pattern for making your own periscope. If you can find all the necessary parts, give it a try.

CONNECTIONS

Mirrors date back to Turkey in around 6000 BCE. They were made of polished obsidian (also called volcanic glass). Later, metal and then glass were used to make mirrors.

But, like Mrs. O'Keefe, people quickly discovered mirrors could be used for more than combing their hair, shaving or putting on makeup. A periscope is

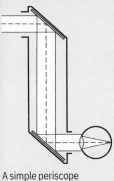

an instrument that allows a person to see around corners. It is made with a long tube and two mirrors, one at each end of the tube. The mirrors sit at a 45-degree angle facing each other. The image from outside is reflected in the first mirror. The image is then reflected down into the second mirror and into the user's eye.

A simple periscope

In the late 1800s, periscopes were used in submarines so sailors could see above the water. During the First World War, periscopes were used by soldiers to look over the tops of the trenches so they could see the enemy without getting shot.

⭐ WHY IS THE MIRROR IMPORTANT IN THIS AREA?

This mirror was probably purchased as an interesting decoration for the wall. Who knows when Mrs. O'Keefe realized she could use it as a type of spyware. We don't know if she hung it in this location because she knew she would be able to see upstairs, or if she discovered it by accident. Perhaps it was never meant for this use, but Mrs. O'Keefe was creative. She created a baby monitor or "nanny cam" long before electricity.

"Nanny-cams" are so small they can be hidden inside the craziest things.

4 OKANAGAN SCIENCE CENTRE

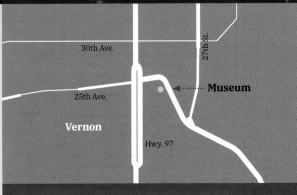

Museum

30th Ave.

25th Ave.

27th St.

Vernon

Hwy. 97

JUST THE FACTS

WHERE IS IT? 2704 Hwy. 6, Vernon, BC, V1T 5G5;
(250) 545-3644
okscience.ca

ARE PHOTOGRAPHS ALLOWED? Yes.

HOW DID IT START? When a group of Boy Scouts travelled to the Pacific Science Center in Seattle, the leader, Bill Sim, was so excited by what he saw, he wanted to create something like it in the Okanagan. He got together with a group of people with a similar goal, and, in 1990, the science centre was founded.

WHERE HAS IT LIVED?

In the beginning, instead of having students come to the centre, the centre went out to the students with a **planetarium** show in an inflatable planetarium. In 1997, the science centre opened in its current location – Park School in Polson Park. Park School is the oldest surviving brick schoolhouse in British Columbia. The school was too small to fit all the exhibits and storage areas, so wings were added to the building.

WHERE DO THE ITEMS COME FROM?

Some of the items are purchased, some are donated and many are built especially for the science centre.

HOW HAS IT CHANGED?

In 1999, the planetarium and space exhibits were designed and constructed for the centre. The centre was renovated in 2001. In 2020, the planetarium technology was upgraded, and new space exhibits were installed. The centre has many travelling exhibits and offers programs that change year to year.

In a museum you can:

learn about species from different biotopes

BITEY MCBITEFACE <u>THE</u> PIRANHA

Bitey is a red-bellied piranha (Pygocentrus nattereri).

He comes from the Amazon River in South America.

Piranhas are polite. After one fish has taken a bite from their prey, it moves to the rear of the school to let others have a turn.

Because the fish are always moving to the back, when piranha are feeding, it looks like the water is boiling.

Bitey is fed twice a week. He likes smelts (little fish) but he spits out vegetables.

In the science centre, you can meet many other fish and reptiles that come from this region.

Piranhas eat mostly other fish and plants, but will eat animals if they are already dead.

JUST THE FACTS

› OKANAGAN SCIENCE CENTRE

GYRO CHAIR

WHAT IS IT? The gyro chair is a piece of equipment that helped astronauts get used to different types of motion while they were in space.

WHAT DOES IT LOOK LIKE? The gyro chair is a large circular frame with a smaller circular frame inside it. Attached to the smaller frame is a chair. The smaller inner frame can spin in all directions.

WHERE DOES IT COME FROM? When Calgary's Telus World of Science was moving, it had some displays it no longer wanted. This gyro chair was one of them. The chair was given to the Okanagan Science Centre.

WHO USED IT? This gyro chair was originally built as a theme park ride. It was taken to different fairs and rodeos around Alberta. Today, at the Okanagan Science Centre, both children and adults love to try the gyro chair.

Photos: Okanagan Science Centre

WOULD YOU BELIEVE?

You might think that spinning and rolling in the gyro chair will make you feel sick to your stomach. You may feel dizzy when you stand up, but you will probably not feel sick. Unlike on a roller coaster, where your stomach sloshes around as you go up and down, on the gyro chair your stomach is basically staying still while your body rotates around it.

Tell Me More

Imagine you are flying a plane. If you make the nose of the plane climb up or dip down, this is called "pitching." If you move the nose of the plane left or right, you would be "yawing." If you rolled the plane over either clockwise or counterclockwise, you would be "rolling." Astronauts need to be able to handle rolling, pitching and yawing when they are in a space capsule, and they must learn how to bring the capsule back to level using control jets.

The gyro chair can roll, pitch and yaw, which is why it is a good training device for astronauts. Unlike this gyro chair, which is controlled by a person spinning it, the gyro chairs used for training astronauts had miniature jets they could control.

You can try out this gyro chair at the science centre. When you are safely strapped into the gyro chair, you will be spun in a circle. If you are feeling okay and you want to try the next stage, you can roll and pitch. The gyro chair only goes as quickly as the person in the chair wants it to go. If you want a real challenge, you can try to write in a notebook with a pen while you are spinning.

My Turn

What do you think would happen if you weren't strapped into the gyro chair? Explain your answer.

Who among your family or friends would be most likely to ride the gyro chair first? Why?

CONNECTIONS

Gyro chairs are a fairly modern invention. However, for thousands of years, human beings have taught themselves to roll, pitch and yaw in the air. We have one picture from ancient Crete, an island in Greece, in which a young person is doing a handspring or flip over a bull.

Today, in southwestern France and northern Spain, athletes (mostly young men) still practise bull leaping. The sport is called *course Landaise*. The athletes leap over cows, not bulls. And they don't put their hands on the animals. They practise different types of flips, meaning they have to know where their bodies are in the air at all times to avoid injury.

All over the world, gymnasts, springboard divers, dancers, snowboarders and figure skaters have to learn similar skills.

⭐ WHY IS THE GYRO CHAIR IMPORTANT IN THIS AREA?

There are very few places in Canada where you can test your skills in a gyro chair. This is one of them.

JUST THE FACTS

WHAT IS IT? A planetarium is a domed structure. Inside the dome an image of stars is projected onto the ceiling.

WHAT DOES IT LOOK LIKE? This planetarium is about five metres in diameter. Twenty adults can sit comfortably on the floor inside the dome.

WHERE DOES IT COME FROM? It was designed and built to fit into the second floor of the science centre's building.

WHO USED IT? Since their invention, planetariums have been used by scientists and teachers to help teach people about the universe.

Thompson/Okanagan
› OKANAGAN SCIENCE CENTRE

BRUCE AIKENHEAD PLANETARIUM

Tell Me More

Big or small, all planetariums have two things in common. They recreate the sky as you might see it on a dark, cloudless night. They do this with a domed screen and a projector. Planetariums and observatories are not the same. Observatories are buildings that have telescopes. Scientists study the stars and planets by looking through these telescopes.

When you visit the science centre planetarium, you will see the sky as it will appear on the night you are there. If you have a question, you can ask it and get an answer immediately. Not only will you learn about the stars as they appear at night, you will hear some stories the Okanagan First Nations have told for thousands of years about those stars.

Bruce Aikenhead designed the planetarium at the Okanagan Science Centre. Before he retired, he was the head of astronauts at the Canadian Space Agency. He even hired Chris Hadfield. Aikenhead also worked on designing the Canadarm, a remote-controlled robotic arm that could lift 30,000 kilograms (about five African elephants) on Earth and 266,000 kilograms (about 44 African elephants) in space.

Photo: Okanagan Science Centre

My Turn

How could you and your family and friends reduce the light pollution around your neighbourhood – or if you live where it is very dark, in neighbourhoods that have light pollution?

CONNECTIONS

The Gottorp Globe
Photo: archer10 (Dennis), Flickr

In the 1600s, sometime after Samuel de Champlain set up a French colony at Quebec City and before the Hudson's Bay Company started in Canada, a German mathematician created the first planetarium. It was a hollow copper globe about three metres in diameter (about one and a half times the length of an average bed). It could seat 12 people. The inside was painted with pictures of the constellations, or groups of stars as they knew them. Each star was made of a gold-coated copper nail head that shone when a lamp was lit inside the globe. The outside of the globe was painted with a map of the known world. This planetarium was called the Gottorp Globe.

WHY IS THE PLANETARIUM IMPORTANT IN THIS AREA?

If it's a clear night, and you still can't see many stars where you live, it might be because of light pollution. When lights from houses, office and apartment buildings, outdoor stadiums and streetlamps light up the sky, we can see only a few of the brightest stars or planets. Planetariums help us imagine what the night sky would look like if there were no lights on Earth. They also allow us to see objects in space that aren't visible to the human eye. Seeing other planets, stars and galaxies helps us understand our place in the universe.

Today, just like in the earliest times on Earth, people make up stories about outer space. We can learn about different cultures through these stories.

This dazzling infrared image from NASA's Spitzer Space Telescope shows hundreds of thousands of stars crowded into the swirling core of our spiral Milky Way galaxy.
Image: NASA/JPL-Caltech/S. Stolovy (Spitzer Science Center/Caltech)

5 OKANAGAN HERITAGE MUSEUM

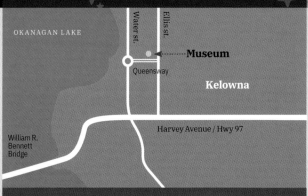

OKANAGAN LAKE

Water st.

Ellis st.

Museum

Queensway

Kelowna

Harvey Avenue / Hwy 97

William R. Bennett Bridge

JUST THE FACTS

WHERE IS IT? 470 Queensway, Kelowna, BC, V1Y 6S7; (250) 763-2417
kelownamuseums.ca

ARE PHOTOGRAPHS ALLOWED? Yes. It's always best if people take photos without a flash. If there is a sacred object that people shouldn't photograph, there will be a sign asking you to please not take a photograph.

HOW DID IT START? In 1925, a group of people interested in history started the Okanagan Historical and Natural History Society. The society began collecting items and displaying them in shop windows.

WHERE HAS IT LIVED?

The museum has lived in a barn loft, a park, even a hotel. The Boy Scouts found display space in a barn loft in 1944. Four years later, it moved to a space in City Park. A new group – the Okanagan Museum and Archives Association – took over and moved the museum first to a building on Kelowna's main street, and then in 1958 to the Willow Inn Lodge near the current bus depot. Nine years later, the collection moved into a single-storey building where the museum now stands. A second storey was added in 1975.

WHERE DO THE ITEMS COME FROM?

Most items have been donated. These days, a committee evaluates all donations. An item should relate to the history of Kelowna and the surrounding area and should be something the museum doesn't already have. The museum also collects a variety of the same object. For example, it has a camera collection, but each camera has something different about it. It could be the make, or the age or something else that sets it apart.

If the museum accepted everything people wanted to donate, it would need to add a few more buildings.

HOW HAS IT CHANGED?

When it started, the museum displayed objects from around the world. Today, the museum tells the cultural, natural and social history of Kelowna and the Okanagan Valley. It works closely with the Westbank First Nation to recognize and honour the valley's Indigenous people.

As well as the permanent collection, the museum has temporary exhibits. You can check them out on the museum's website.

learn about animals

BEAVER SKELETON

The beaver's forepaws are similar to human hands, but without thumbs.

Even without thumbs, they can fold leaves before putting them into their mouths.

The scientific name for this beaver is Castor canadensis.

Beavers pelts were important to fur traders .

Fur traders and trappers depended on the syilx/ Okanagan people for horses and food, as well as guiding and packing services.

The tail (missing from this skeleton) is made of skinny tail bones covered by skin, fat and muscle.

The beaver uses its tail to move through the water and to balance when it is sitting on its back legs.

JUST THE FACTS

WHAT IS IT? Protected by a display case is an adult grizzly bear, also known as a North American brown bear (Ursus arctos).

WHAT DOES IT LOOK LIKE? If the bear were standing on its back legs, it would be approximately 2.13 metres tall. So, if this grizzly bear stretched out on your bed, its feet would hang over the end. He weighed 227 kilograms. He was so heavy you wouldn't want him sleeping in the top bunk of a bunk bed, especially if you were on the bottom.

WHERE DOES IT COME FROM? The museum purchased the bear in 1995.

WHO USED IT? We do not know anything about the hunter who killed this bear.

Thompson/Okanagan
> **OKANAGAN HERITAGE MUSEUM**

GRIZZLY BEAR

Tell Me More

If you met this guy in the woods, you wouldn't be able to study him. In fact, you definitely wouldn't want to! Many of us will never have the chance to see in nature some of the wildlife found in the museum. When a museum puts an animal on display, we can learn about where that animal lives, its habits and also the impact humans have had on the species. Being able to see a grizzly bear up close without being in danger is amazing. Compare your hand to its paw. How long are its claws compared to your fingers? How big are its teeth?

kiláwna? · Grizzly Bear

❓ WOULD YOU BELIEVE?

Grizzly bears are known for their long claws. But in the fall, bears' claws are half the length they are in the spring when they come out of hibernation. That's because bears use their claws for digging and, over the months they are awake, their claws wear down.

Stories about bears are found in many cultures. In Roman myth, a **nymph** named Callisto made the goddess Juno very angry and the goddess turned Callisto into a bear. Callisto had a young son who grew up not knowing who his mother was. One day, he was out hunting and came across a bear. Of course, he did not know it was his mother, but somehow she recognized him. The boy was just about to kill his mother when Jupiter, the head of all the gods, stopped him and turned both mother and son into constellations – groups of stars – one that looks like a big bear, and one that looks like a small bear. Callisto became Ursa (the Latin word for bear) Major, her son, Ursa Minor.

Callisto, almost killed by her own son

My Turn

Find a map, graph or chart of grizzly bear habitat in British Columbia in the 1990s and a map, graph or chart of their habitat today. How are they different? Why has there been a change?

⭐ WHY IS THE GRIZZLY IMPORTANT IN THIS AREA?

Kelowna comes from the nsyilxcən word for grizzly bear: *kiláwnaʔ*. When an early settler, August Gillard, first came to the valley, the local syilx/Okanagan people gave him one of their *q̓ʷc̓iʔ* (winter homes). Gillard was a big man with lots of hair both on his head and on his face. He wore a bearskin jacket to keep warm. Unlike the Okanagan people who bathed daily, Gillard didn't believe in bathing, and, you can imagine, he became very stinky.

A very stinky early settler, **August Gillard**

Photo: Kelowna Public Archives: KPA#5728

Most men entered and exited their *q̓ʷc̓iʔ* through the top, but Gillard crawled out through the narrow ground-level entrance usually used by women, older people and children. When he did, the local people thought he looked and smelled like a grizzly bear coming out of its den. They called him *kiláwnaʔ*. When the town needed a name, several people remembered Gillard's story and chose a word that sounded much like the nsyilxcən word for grizzly bear: **Kelowna.**

JUST THE FACTS

WHAT IS IT? This millstone was used to grind soya beans to make tofu.

WHAT DOES IT LOOK LIKE? The millstone is in two pieces, the headstone and the base. The headstone sits on top of the base. What you can't see in the museum is the large copper hopper that stood on top of the headstone. The hopper held 3.6 kilograms (or eight pounds) of soaked soya beans. A slow drip of water was introduced as the beans were ground. The liquified product flowed into the channel that runs around the base, out the spout and into a pail.

WHERE DOES IT COME FROM? When the Wong family home at 245 Leon Avenue was sold, the family donated the millstone to the museum.

WHO USED IT? Wong Ying and his wife Sue Lee Ping Wong used the millstone. They made tofu with this millstone to help support their family of 11 children.

Thompson/Okanagan

› OKANAGAN HERITAGE MUSEUM

MILLSTON

Headstone

Base

Tell Me More

Would you get up at four in the morning to make tofu? After her husband died in 1965, Sue Lee Ping Wong worked on her own to produce tofu or bean cakes. Today, many vegetarians eat tofu instead of meat, but it wasn't as popular in the 1960s and '70s. The first step was to grind soaked soya beans using the motorized millstone. Grinding the soya beans was only one step in a long process that took two to three hours for a batch of eight dozen tofu. On some busy weekends, Mrs. Wong would be making tofu for 10 to 12 hours a day.

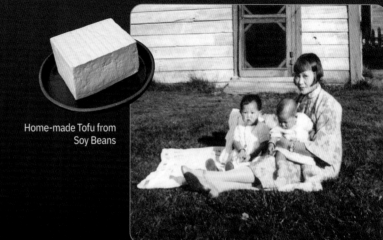

Home-made Tofu from Soy Beans

WOULD YOU BELIEVE?

One of the restaurants that ordered tofu from Mrs. Wong was the Goon Hong restaurant. It ordered 24 – 30 dozen tofu cakes a week. Unfortunately, the restaurant was 52 kilometres away in Vernon. In order to get the tofu to Vernon, a trusted Royal Canadian Mounted Police (RCMP) officer picked up pails each holding eight dozen tofu from Mrs. Wong and, while performing his highway patrol duties, dropped them off in Vernon.

Chocolate is made from grinding cacao beans. Making chocolate goes back to 1500 BCE and the Olmecs of southern Mexico. They used a grinding stone to make a paste from the roasted beans. Unlike Mrs. Wong, who used a mechanized grinding wheel, early chocolate makers ground the beans by hand. The person grinding the beans used a heavy stone. It was shaped like a cylinder, sort of like a rolling pin, and rolled over the beans to crush them. The grinding stone – which was rectangular, not round like Mrs. Wong's stone – was often heated by a small fire underneath to keep the cacao beans soft and easier to make into paste.

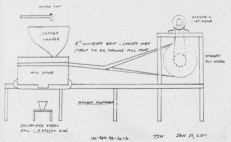

Sue Lee Wong's millstone setup

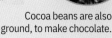

Cocoa beans are also ground, to make chocolate.

My Turn

There are many recipes for main courses and desserts using tofu. Find one you can make with an adult or by yourself (if you are allowed), and try it out on your family or friends.

WHY IS THE MILLSTONE IMPORTANT IN THIS AREA?

Mrs. Wong's millstone is a symbol of the challenges faced by the Chinese who encountered racist policies in Canada. To reduce the number of Chinese immigrants coming to Canada, the federal government created a "head tax." In 1885, every Chinese person coming into Canada paid $50 to the government. By 1903, that amount had increased to $500. In 1911, the population of Kelowna was approximately 1,650, including over 100 Chinese – most of whom were men. It was very hard for Chinese men to save enough money to bring their wives and families to Canada. Due to provincial laws, Chinese were not allowed to work in certain jobs, so the men mostly worked in low-paying jobs in orchards, on farms, in restaurants, laundries and stores. In 1923, the Canadian Government passed the Chinese Immigration Act (also known as the Chinese Exclusion Act), which banned the immigration of Chinese into Canada. This act existed until 1947.

Kelowna's Chinatown has all but disappeared. Mrs. Wong's soya millstone reminds us of the ways the Chinese who came to Kelowna contributed to the city.

6 SNCƏWIPS HERITAGE MUSEUM

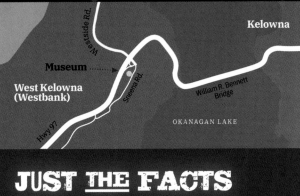

Kelowna

Westside Rd.

Museum ·········

West Kelowna
(Westbank)

Sneena Rd.

William R. Bennett
Bridge

OKANAGAN LAKE

Hwy 97

JUST THE FACTS

WHERE IS IT? Okanagan Lake Shopping Centre, 525 BC-97, West Kelowna, BC, V1Z 4C9; (778) 755-2787
sncəwips.com

ARE PHOTOGRAPHS ALLOWED? Yes.

HOW DID IT START? In 2005, when Westbank First Nation community achieved self-government, they asked their community what their concerns were. They said language and cultural revitalization, as well as repatriation of their cultural artifacts and ancestral remains. They strongly supported the creation of a museum or cultural centre.

First they created a repository – which means a place where items are stored. It was recognized by the government, which allowed them to bring back their belongings from around the world. They found all sorts of things: paintings, baskets, tools. Soon the collection was big. They asked the community again if they still supported starting a museum. The answer was yes.

WHERE HAS IT LIVED?

In 2014, before the new museum opened to the public, members were given a preview to ensure the organizer's vision met with their approval. In the past, sharing First Nations history and cultural practices was sometimes abused and had been hurtful. But museum organizers believe having a museum is important. "This is our history, it's our responsibility to claim our place in the Okanagan."

WHERE DO THE ITEMS COME FROM?

Some First Nations people find the terms "artifact" or "object" problematic. They prefer the word "belongings." It connects the item back to the original source of ownership, reminding us that the things we see in museums were often taken without permission. Items come to the museum in different ways. Sometimes the Chief and Council representatives buy them on behalf of the community, or Non-Indigenous people inherit objects and offer them to the museum. Other items are loaned by Nation members.

If the bones of First Nations people are discovered they are taken by the museum and treated in a way that has been established by their Nation, making sure their ancestors are respected. They will never be displayed and will always be reburied and laid to rest. Occasionally the museum is given objects from another territory, If this happens, they contact that territory and ask if it wants the item returned. If so, the item is repatriated – returned. If not, the museum keeps it for display.

HOW HAS IT CHANGED?

The museum recently moved to new bigger and brighter space with more room for exhibits and art.

Learn how to fish with reeds
FISHING WEIR | nsyilxcəːʷsxwlikn

It's made with red willow (Salix laevigata). Willows are incredibly flexible. The weir needs this quality in order to maintain its shape.

The glue that kept everything in place was pine pitch.

When it's dry, this weir weighs about the same as a plastic laundry basket. Add some water and the trap doubles in size. It takes several men to drag it to shore when it's full of fish.

Traditionally, families made the weir as a team – women, children and Elders.

Students from Sensisyusten West Bank Okanagan immersion school made the weir on a field trip. (Sensisyusten is an Okanagan word that means "house of learning.")

It's 200 centimetres (or two metres) long. Think ten brand new, eraser-tipped pencils balanced on top of each other.

To the fish the weir looks like a place they might find food. They slip through the first chamber and are then locked in the second chamber. It works like a funnel, gradually narrowing.

The Okanagan people had strict beliefs about the amount of fish that could be caught. They believed in only taking what they needed and sharing with everyone. Everybody in the community was to be cared for and well fed.

JUST THE FACTS

WHAT IS IT? This is a canoe carved from a black cottonwood tree.

WHAT DOES IT LOOK LIKE? It is 5.8 metres long. That's about the size of a giraffe lying on its side, or half as tall as a telephone pole. It takes six strong people with muscles the size of bowling balls to lift it. Four passengers can fit in it.

WHERE DOES IT COME FROM? Master carver Gordon Marchand took on the project after learning he'd been diagnosed with cancer. He built this canoe especially for the Westbank First Nation community. The practice of making dugout canoes had almost fallen out of use because of the Indian Act of 1876. This unjust and tragic act was created to wipe out First Nations' culture in order to promote Euro-Canadian society. Gordon still had this knowledge and felt a strong urge to pass on the art of making a dugout canoe. This kind of skill is so specialized that Gordon filmed himself building the canoe. The film is kept in the museum's archives. Gordon passed away in 2009 from cancer, but his son Frank and his colleague Marvin Lewis continue Gordon's legacy.

WHO USED IT? In the past, these canoes were the family minivan. The First People of the Okanagan used them for activities like trading trips and visiting with friends. While birch bark canoes were mostly used in the Penticton area, in the Westbank area, dense wetlands required stronger, more durable dugout canoes.

BLACK COTTONWOOD CANOE

nsyilxcə: x̌ʔiʔ\

Tell Me More

On the front of the canoe, master carver Gordon Marchand carved a bear with a frog in its mouth. For the syilx/Okanagan people, the bear is known for its human-like characteristics. The syilx people learned what plants they could use for medicine by watching what a sick bear would eat.

Frogs also have a special significance in Okanagan culture. Frog Woman (swarakxn t'kaɬmixʷ) is a traveller and never leaves the water. She's powerful. Depending on how she's treated, she can be good or bad.

Black cottonwood (mulx) is the material of choice for this kind of canoe. The Okanagan people have been using this wood for hundreds of years. It's very tough and can handle waterways that are rough and full of rocks.

These days, black cottonwood ecosystems are at risk in the Okanagan. This tree once grew all over the area where the museum now stands. In 2017, to honour Canada's 150th birthday, community members planted 150 cottonwood trees in areas throughout the Okanagan. The purpose of the project was to highlight the tree's role in Indigenous culture and to contribute to environmental stewardship in local waterways.

WOULD YOU BELIEVE?

This canoe actually leaves the museum to go on fishing trips and adventures. That's not all. It plays a major role in the local Canada Day parade. It floats very well, but it tends to veer left. Paddlers require two types of paddles for this canoe. A rounded paddle is used for routine steering and travelling, whereas a pointy paddle is used for taking off and navigating rocky areas.

My Turn

Imagine if you could carve something on your family's vehicle, what would it be? What creature would you pick as your family's symbol? Take a piece of paper and draw your carving out.

⭐ WHY IS THE CANOE IMPORTANT IN THIS AREA?

The waterways were the Okanagan First Nation's highways and without a strong canoe to travel in they'd be stuck at home. Water is also sacred to the Okanagan. Many of their physical, cultural and spiritual practices are connected to the local waterways.

CONNECTIONS

Maori, the Indigenous people of New Zealand, use a boat propelled by paddlers. It's called a *waka*. These range in size from small fishing vessels to large vessels used by warriors. They can be twice the size of the black cottonwood canoe.

Maori *waka*. photo: W. Bulach, Wikimedia Commons

JUST THE FACTS

CRADLEBOARD

/nsyilxcə Mx̌ʷal-

WHAT IS IT? Officially, this cradleboard is 60.96 centimetres long, the length of a kid's snowshoe. At first glance, it looks heavy, but it's light. It weighs about the same as two cans of pop. If you put a baby in it, that's a different story. Some babies are heavier than others. A newborn weighs about eight to ten cans of pop. An average three-month-old baby about 14 cans of pop. Add two more cans for an average six-month-old, and so on...

WHAT DOES IT LOOK LIKE? Margaret Eli made the cradleboard in 1972 for her daughter Buffy Eli, now De Guevara, who then used it to carry her daughter, Summer De Guevara. This piece reflects the time period it was created in. The frame is built with wood and covered with corduroy and denim. Back then, these materials were very trendy.

WHERE DOES IT COME FROM? It was gifted to the museum by members of the Eli and De Guevara families. It awaits the next generation. If a member of the family needs it, the cradleboard leaves the museum and is returned when the baby has outgrown it.

WHO USED IT? Some people think cradleboards were worn on the mother's back, but this isn't true. Okanagan women worked primarily as root diggers. This is hard work that involves a lot of leaning over. Mothers rested their babies in cradleboards against trees while they worked nearby. There were lots of benefits to this, including allowing the mother and baby to stay close throughout the day, making both of them happy. Another added benefit was that the baby was exposed to the world with the security of their mother close by.

WOULD YOU BELIEVE?

The cradleboard is a useful and flexible piece of equipment. Not only can it be leaned against almost anything, it can be bounced to comfort the baby and swung to put the baby to sleep. It's also a great shelter. The head piece works like an umbrella or the hood of a baby carriage to protect the baby from too much wind, rain, snow or sun.

Tell Me More

Why this fabric was used for this cradleboard is more complicated than just style. Traditionally, the cradleboard would have been made of animal hides. But at that time the Okanagan people weren't allowed to hunt or fish because of an unjust law known as the Indian Act. The goal of this was to make First Nations people give up on their traditions and act like the European settlers.

The act was a form of discrimination. That's a pretty complicated word. *Kid's Britannica* defines "discrimination" as the "unfair treatment of one particular person or group of people...Discrimination based on race is called racism."

Nowadays, young mothers are free to build cradleboards from anything they want. These days, they'd probably choose more sustainable materials – hides are again popular. Most cradleboards are still handed down from generation to generation, so there's usually no need to make new ones.

When babies outgrew their cradleboards and became toddlers, they were given to Grandma to look after. If you've ever looked after a toddler, you'll know why. It's impossible to get anything done while you're running after a curious toddler.

My Turn

Pretend to be a journalist and think of five questions you'd ask your parents or caregivers about how you were cared for as a baby. Remember to include the five *W*'s and one *H*. Record or film your interview and make your own news show.

CONNECTIONS

At Mountain Equipment Co-op, a Canadian outdoor shop, parents can buy an assortment of carriers that look like they are based on a cradleboard. These come with a kickstand so there's no need for a tree.

WHY IS THE CRADLEBOARD IMPORTANT IN THIS AREA?

Cradleboards are a major connection to the past, an ancient tradition that still carries on as part of modern-day family life in the Okanagan community. Nowadays, however, you're just as likely to find a cradleboard leaning up against a dishwasher as a tree.

Cradleboards are used in some other Indigenous cultures as well. This is a Skolt Sami woman (Finland) and her child.
Photo: Wikimedia Commons, Eino Mäkinen

7 SUMMERLAND MUSEUM AND ARCHIVES SOCIETY

Museum

Summerland

JUST THE FACTS

WHERE IS IT? 9521 Wharton Street, Summerland, BC, V0H 1Z0; (250) 494-9395
summerlandmuseum.org

ARE PHOTOGRAPHS ALLOWED? Yes.

HOW DID IT START? The Summerland Museum and Archives is the creation of the Summerland Museum Group, which began working together in 1965. This was the very same year that Queen Elizabeth II proclaimed the Maple Leaf our national flag, Toronto's famous City Hall opened and the Guess Who – one of the first Canadian rock bands to be known internationally – formed in Winnipeg. At first the museum group didn't have a museum space, so it kept the artifacts it found in the members' homes. The group met regularly to discuss its dream of opening a museum.

WHERE HAS IT LIVED?

It took the group years to find the ideal space for its museum. For a short time, the museum was housed in a small, cement-block space attached to the old Summerland arena, but when this was demolished, the museum was forced to find a new home and all its belongings were put back in storage. The second museum was housed at the Kettle Valley Railway (KVR) station. This didn't work out because it was too far from the centre of town.

Finally, in 1984, the same year as pop singer Avril Lavigne was born and the Edmonton Oilers won their first Stanley Cup, the museum found a permanent home in a building created especially for it by the municipality.

WHERE DO THE ITEMS COME FROM?

The museum collects donations that tell the story of Summerland, its surroundings and the people who live there. On its website it has a list of the kind of items it is on the lookout for. In 2006, the museum was gifted an important collection of art by its former director, Doreen Tait.

HOW HAS IT CHANGED?

Today, the museum has a fabulous website filled with information about Summerland's history. Here, one can learn about the town's early settlers, read a letter by a local First World War soldier or read about what it was like to come to Summerland as a war bride. War brides were women, mostly from the United Kingdom, who married Canadian soldiers during the Second World War. Many of them were very surprised by life in their new country.

In a museum you can:

travel forgotten routes

KETTLE VALLEY STATION

This station is a reproduction of the West Summerland train station that was built in 1916, a stop on the Kettle Valley Railway's route from Midway to Vancouver.

The Kettle Valley Railway was the only direct link to the coast for the people of the town.

People from all walks of life waited in the station as they prepared for their journey on the Kettle Valley Railway. It was probably a hub of activity and filled with chatter.

The trains benefitted the agriculture industry that made up a large part of Summerland's economy.

Back in 1915, when the first trains began running from Summerland to Vancouver, the journey took 23 hours and 20 minutes. How many times do you think the average kid asked, "Are we there yet?"

Today, visitors can ride on locomotive No. 3716, a restored steam train on a small part of the Summerland KVR. This ride starts at a station called Prairie Valley. The journey is 90 minutes.

Between 1961 and 1989 the Kettle Valley Railway was abandoned.

There are 27 countries that don't have railways. Common reasons countries don't have a railway include lack of funding, a difficult environment, size and competition from automobiles.

Time to Wonder

JUST THE FACTS

WHAT IS IT? The tent house looks like small house, but its roof is made out of canvas like a tent. It's a hybrid like those trailers with the canvas pop-outs. This tent house is a composite made by the museum. It represents the tent houses used by settlers, like the Blewitt family of Summerland, around 1907.

WHAT DOES IT LOOK LIKE? The Blewitt tent house was about 4 x 8 metres in size. It was put together with a wooden frame, wooden sides, wooden floors and a double canvas roof. It was divided with sheets. The floors were carpeted, and a box heater heated the house. To say it could be chilly when the winter wind blew is an understatement. The Blewitt's house had a small add-on kitchen.

CAN YOU IMAGINE LIVING IN A HOUSE LIKE THIS WITH YOUR FAMILY? It's about the same size as a VW camper van. Do you think you'd all get along?

WHERE DOES IT COME FROM? Julien Butler, the museum's curator, isn't sure who built the replica of the tent house.

WHO USED IT? The Blewitt family is a good example of the kind of people that came to Summerland. They arrived in Summerland from Hartney on the Souris River in Manitoba.

Jack Blewett, who was a grist miller and a millwright, worked in the local flour mill. Jack and his wife, Mary, were originally from Lakefield, Ontario. The couple and their two children, Gordon and Jean, decided to move to Summerland after Jack was diagnosed with a serious illness and the doctor recommended a milder climate.

TENT HOUSE

Most tent houses like the Blewitt's had no electricity, plumbing or running water.

Tell Me More

Tent houses came in all sorts of shapes and sizes. Some were fancy, while others were simple. The Blewitt family lived in a tent house on a lot in a peach orchard. These lots cost between $275 and $300. Most of the lots were wooded and boggy. When the weather was good, the canvas walls rolled up on the Blewitt's tent house, so it was like living outside. At first the house didn't have protection from rain and the family placed umbrellas and oilskins over their beds on wet days. Later, they added a fly tent and it was more comfortable. This kind of tent doesn't have walls and hangs over the main structure. People use them to keep tents as dry as possible.

Photos this page: Summerland Museum and Archives Society

My Turn

Write a letter from the **perspective** of a kid living in a tent house watching their family build their first house. Now write a letter from the perspective of a kid living in the first colony on Mars. What does your temporary home there look like?

CONNECTIONS

The Mongolian *ger*, like the tent house, is made out of material that is flexible and nonpermanent. It is believed nomadic Mongolians have used gers as their homes since they began keeping animals. Traditionally, the ger is round, made out of felt and portable. It's held together with wooden poles.

Gers only have one door, which is usually beautifully decorated, painted in orange or blue. The doors always face south. There are no windows. There's a round hole at the top that serves as the chimney. Each ger has a stove in the middle of it.

Nomadic families live this way throughout Mongolia. Families of all sizes live together in gers. There are no walls, so there's no privacy.

⭐ WHY IS THE TENT HOUSE IMPORTANT IN THIS AREA?

The tent house was very popular with Summerland's settlers. Families lived in them while they worked on their permanent houses. In the Okanagan, which was known as the "California of Canada," people could live in them all year round.

JUST THE FACTS

VELOCIPEDI

WHAT IS IT? The velocipede was a piece of equipment used by railways to inspect the tracks.

WHAT DOES IT LOOK LIKE? This three-wheeled piece of railway equipment looks as if it belongs in a modern art gallery or on a film set, not travelling along a railway track. The three wheels kept the machine secured to the track without the extra weight of a fourth wheel. The machine needed to be as light as possible as the drivers might want to go over a piece of track again or turn around. This velocipede is made out of wood and is bright yellow.

WHERE DOES IT COME FROM? It was used in Grand Forks by track watchers in the 20th century. It was given to the museum by the "Victoria Museum" (probably the Royal BC Museum).

WHO USED IT? The velocipede was used by railway track inspectors. This clever machinery allowed the inspectors to cover great distances quickly while they examined the track for damage and deterioration. Most importantly, it kept them close to the track, making it easier to spot problems like cracked or broken rails, track distortion, misalignment and pumping ties that needed repairs.

Photo: Summerland Museum and Archives Society

WOULD YOU BELIEVE?

The Palmerston Railway Heritage Museum in Ontario holds handcar races each year. The raceway travels in front of the museum and under the town's long pedestrian bridge – the longest pedestrian bridge in all of Ontario. Each team consists of four pumpers and one pusher. The cars weigh about 362.9 kilograms and can travel as fast as 15.6 metres per second. This unusual event attracts visitors from across Canada.

Tell Me More

The velocipede's inventor, George Sheffield, lived on a farm near the Michigan Central Railroad in Three Rivers, Michigan. Every day he walked along the tracks back and forth from work. It was during these walks that he came up with the idea of creating the velocipede.

In 1877, he built his first velocipede, testing it at night so he wouldn't get into trouble with railway officials for illegally using the tracks. One night as he was out, he discovered a broken rail. He flagged down an oncoming train, saving the train and the people in it from certain disaster. This was great, but it did mean his secret was revealed. George didn't need to worry. As a reward, he was allowed to test out the velocipede on the stretch of track from his farm to Three Rivers. The velocipede ran by using both foot pedals and handles, an odd mixture of pushing and pulling the handle back and forth while at the same time pedalling it like a bike. This method of driving made it easy to control the speed.

News of George's invention spread, and the railway approached him and asked him to build some velocipedes. In 1879, the velocipede received Patent No. 213,254.

My Turn

George Sheffield was inspired to create the velocipede by paying attention to his surroundings as he walked home from work every day. Next time you come home from school, take a moment to reflect on your environment. What do you see that needs changing? What might you invent to help your community?

CONNECTIONS

Did you know "the velocipede" is also a term used to describe forerunners of the modern bicycle? What do these two vehicles have in common? Both of these vehicles use human energy, are propelled by pedals and/or cranks and have one or more wheels.

WHY IS THE VELOCIPEDE IMPORTANT IN THIS AREA?

When the Kettle Valley Railway finally arrived in the Okanagan around 1915, it changed everything as service included both passenger and freight trains. People could now visit friends and family as far away as Vancouver and Medicine Hat. It was good news for businesses too. Freight carried from the region included ore from the Kootenays, as well as forestry products and fruit from the Okanagan. Of course, it also meant finished products could be delivered into the area. The velocipede was an important part of this as it made it possible for the inspectors to keep a close eye on the tracks for possible problems.

8 PENTICTON MUSEUM & ARCHIVES

WHERE HAS IT LIVED?

The museum moved to the Penticton Community Art complex next to the city library in 1965.

WHERE DO THE ITEMS COME FROM?

Over the years, the collection that started with Atkins has grown considerably. The museum's main source is private donations. The museum has a collecting **mandate** that governs what it collects. One recent donation was from Barrie Sanford, a Canadian railway historian, who specializes

in the history of the Kettle Valley Railway, which was headquartered in Penticton. This collection consists of the working diaries, business papers and photographs from the personal collection of Andrew McCulloch, the chief engineer of the KVR.

The donation confirms the Penticton Museum & Archives as the most important destination for railway scholars interested in the KVR.

HOW HAS IT CHANGED?

The museum is always changing. One of the biggest changes was the introduction of the Hands-on Heritage Lab in 2018. This interactive area took two years to create and is very popular with parents and children.

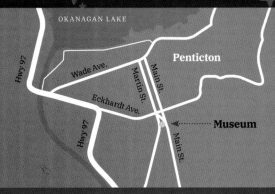

JUST THE FACTS

WHERE IS IT? 785 Main Street, Penticton, BC, V2A 5E3; (250) 490-2451
pentictonmuseum.com

ARE PHOTOGRAPHS ALLOWED? Yes.

HOW DID IT START? In 1954, local historian and collector R. N. Atkinson was given permission to display his collection on an old decommissioned sternwheeler, the SS *Sicamous*. Over the years, the Penticton resident and First World War veteran had accumulated a wide range of militaria (items related to the military), native artifacts, firearms and antiques.

In the 1920s, he ran a private museum from his home. Today, the temporary gallery is named in his honour. He was the Penticton Museum's first curator.

GREAT BASIN GOPHER SNAKE

The museum's Great Basin gopher snake (Pituophis catenifer deserticola) is named Lawrence, and is about 4 or 5 years old, and lives at the Penticton Museum.

The species is native to the Okanagan, Thompson, Similkameen, Kettle Creek, Fraser and Nicola valleys in BC.

His mouth is small and a little upturned at the corners, so it looks a little like Lawrence is smiling.

This species is vulnerable. It's considered open to dangers like habitat loss.

Lawrence is often mistaken for a rattlesnake, but his patterning is really quite different. Sadly, many nonvenomous gopher snakes have lost their lives because of this similarity.

He was donated by the BC Wildlife Park, which got him from the Canada Border Services Agency. This snake is too used to living with people to survive in his natural habitat.

Its hibernacula – where it sleeps in the winter – is often disturbed when people build roads and do landscaping. Cars and trains also often kill these snakes, as they like to sun themselves on roads and tracks.

Gopher snakes kill their prey by squeezing the breath out of them. But this snake can't hunt for himself. So the museum staff buys frozen dead mice for him. Lawerence doesn't like his dinner frozen – who does? Before he's served, the staff let the mouse thaw. Once the mouse is warmed up, the snake can smell it and knows dinner is on its way.

Biologists say these snakes are fabulous at pest control on farms, vineyards and orchards as they eat mice and rats.

These snakes are the largest in British Colombia. This one is approximately 1.5 metres long.

JUST THE FACTS

› PENTICTON MUSEUM & ARCHIVES

PENNY FARTHING

WHAT IS IT? This is a black Penny Farthing bicycle from 1896. These bicycles were also known as the High Wheel, High Wheeler and Ordinary. They were invented by the British inventor James Starley, who is now considered the father of the bicycle industry. The bikes were sturdy and built to last.

WHAT DOES IT LOOK LIKE? The Penny Farthing is the height of an average fridge. It has a huge front wheel that is about 1.5 metres tall. The much smaller back wheel is about the size of the large wheel on a tricycle. The rider sits on a saddle high up, almost over the front wheel. The handlebars are straight and not very wide. The thinking behind the strange shape of the bike was that this would make it easier and smoother to ride.

WHERE DOES IT COME FROM? This bicycle was donated to the museum by the family of Robert (Bob) Lee Livingston in his memory.

WHO USED IT? Penticton resident Bob Livingston rode the bike. Bob was known for his impressive photograph collection of antique and specialty vehicles. In his spare time, he restored antique cars and trucks. One of his prized possessions was a modified super stock car. He enjoyed racing it in Victoria, Langley, and Yakima and Wenatchee in Washington state.

The Penny Farthing was a big bike!
Photo: Major James Skitt Matthews , City of Vancouver Archives

WHY IS THE PENNY FARTHING IMPORTANT IN THIS AREA?

Bob was known in Penticton as the man in the bowler hat and a cigar in his hand, who waved at the public as he rode his Penny Farthing in the Peach Festival parade and other local celebrations.

Tell Me More

In his teens, Bob performed in the circus, entertaining audiences with motorcycle tricks. This kind of coordination probably was the reason he was able to learn how to ride the Penny Farthing. These bikes were notoriously dangerous. Getting on and off one required balance and bravery. At the height of their popularity, a few Penny Farthing enthusiasts died just trying to mount the bike. After all, it's quite a distance to fall.

There were many accidents and deaths. Riders didn't have much control. When going downhill, they were supposed to stop pedalling and rest their feet on the handlebars. It's no wonder that when Starley's nephew invented the Rover Safety bicycle with a lower saddle the Penny Farthing lost its popularity.

My Turn

Do you have the balance needed to ride a Penny Farthing? Try timing yourself while standing on one leg on an unstable object like a pillow or a rock or a ball. Record your time and practise to see if you can improve.

CONNECTIONS

Would you believe that riding bikes helped the progress of women's rights? The game changer was a bike known as the Safety Bike. It was the first bike women were allowed to use. Before the Safety Bike, women didn't have much freedom when it came to moving around. Depending on their class standing in society, they were expected to travel by foot though never alone, by horse but only sidesaddle, and by carriage. Women of wealth were to be supervised in their travels by a chaperone – an older, responsible, generally married woman. A bike was freeing as they could ride quickly. Plus, there was no room for a bossy chaperone, parents and big skirts.

Some men hated women riding bikes. They tried to stop it by saying some pretty crazy things like it would give women an unpleasant look known as "bicycle face" as they learned to ride, or make them bowlegged from pedalling. They even went as far as to say it would give them **tuberculosis**.

This drawing shows a penny farthing and a safety bicycle.
Image: Wikimedia Commons, Kolossos

JUST THE FACTS

PRIVATE KENYON'S SWEATER

WHAT IS IT? This is a sweater worn by Canadian soldier Private H. S. Kenyon of the 29th Battalion of Vancouver when he was a prisoner of war in a German camp during the First World War.

WHAT DOES IT LOOK LIKE? It is an average-sized man's antique woolen sweater hand-knit in basket stitch with a large cable stitch in the front. The body of the sweater is green and grey. The wool looks as if it's been doubled up. It has a large collar in a rusty orange colour.

WHERE DOES IT COME FROM? The sweater is on loan from Private Kenyon's family. It's part of a tribute at the museum in honour of John "Jack" Babcock. At the age of 109, Babcock was the last surviving Canadian veteran of the Great War. This homage also acknowledges the collective memories of the Penticton family members who served.

WHO USED IT? Private Gordon Mellest, a friend of Private H. S. Kenyon, knit the sweater. They were imprisoned together. Private Mellest got the wool by unravelling the scarves and socks sent by the Canadian Red Cross to prisoners of war. Private Kenyon wore the sweater to disguise himself as a civilian on his fourth and ultimately successful escape from the camp.

John "Jack" Babcock. At the age of 109, Babcock was the last surviving Canadian veteran of the Great War.
Wikimedia Commons

54

WOULD YOU BELIEVE?

Once he was out of the army, Private Kenyon started a construction business in Penticton called Kenyon and Company. He worked on many important local buildings like the United Church on Main Street, the city hall, the original part of the Penticton Trade and Convention Centre and the library and museum. Today, one of his great-grandsons still works in Penticton construction.

My Turn

Private Kenyon kept a diary, which is why we know so much about his life during the war. Have you ever kept one? This week keep a diary. Write a paragraph a day. Who knows who might read it in the future?

WHY IS PRIVATE KENYON'S SWEATER IMPORTANT IN THIS AREA?

At first view, the visitor sees a familiar piece of clothing, similar to something that a friend might knit today. This item represents something more – a link between the past and the present. The sweater is a concrete reminder that history is real, and that war doesn't just happen to other people. It affected people who lived in our community, like Private Kenyon.

CONNECTIONS

In Canada, there were prison camps during the First World War for interned civilians. After the war started, private citizens, particularly new immigrants who had historical ties with countries like Germany, Turkey and the Austro-Hungarian Empire, were considered a threat to Canadian security. Many of the men of military age from these groups were detained in work camp facilities on the prairies and places like Fort Henry, in Kingston, Ontario, and Vernon, BC. There were 24 camps across Canada.

Most of the civilian camps closed in 1917, before the end of the war. This was because Canada was in need of male workers, especially in agriculture and industry, with so many men away at war. Many of the men in the labour camps were experienced in these areas.

Tell Me More

Private H. S. Kenyon was captured on April 19, 1916, during the Battle of St. Eloi Craters. According to the *Canadian Encyclopedia*, "It was the first major engagement for the 2nd Canadian Division." The battle was a terrible loss for Canada and our allies. That night, 41 prisoners were taken. These men were put in different groups to work for the Germans.

Private Kenyon was placed in a group with six other Canadian soldiers. The treatment by the German guards was brutal, according to Private Kenyon. He said the guards hit their prisoners with the butts of their rifles for the slightest disobedience.

British Columbia housed prisoners of war in six camps during WW1. Most of them were in the Interior.

Revelstoke

Vernon

Monashee-Mara Lake

Edgewood

Penticton

Fernie

9

PRINCETON & DISTRICT MUSEUM & ARCHIVES

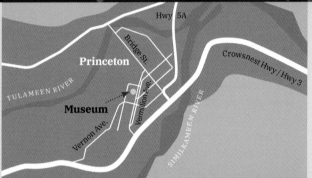

Hwy 5A

Bridge St.

Princeton

Crowsnest Hwy / Hwy 3

TULAMEEN RIVER

Vermilion Ave.

Museum

SIMILKAMEEN RIVER

Vernon Ave.

JUST THE FACTS

WHERE IS IT? 167 Vermilion Avenue, Princeton, BC, V0X 1W0; (250) 295-7588
princetonmuseum.org

ARE PHOTOGRAPHS ALLOWED? Yes.

HOW DID IT START? In 1958, three women from the Princeton area decided it would be nice to have a museum and began scouting for artifacts and a location. Eventually, they found a space, an old log cabin once used by a local miner. The original museum was called Princeton Pioneer Museum. It wasn't until the 1980s that the name was changed to Princeton & District Museum & Archives.

The first museum had a huge sign over the entranceway, a bearskin decorating the front wall and antlers over the window. In the yard, there was an old stagecoach for visitors to look at.

WHERE HAS IT LIVED?

In 1967, Princeton celebrated Canada's centennial by building a space for the museum and library to share. The museum is still housed there today, though it's gone through many changes. Throughout the years, the museum's collection has continued to grow. Today, the museum boasts a vast collection of photographs of early pioneers, as well as First Nations' belongings.

WHERE DO THE ITEMS COME FROM?

Many of the museum's fabulous artifacts were donated by locals.

HOW HAS IT CHANGED?

In 1999, the museum expanded once more, adding the Joe Pollard Wing. This wing was created especially to house the museum's 40,000 **fossils** and minerals. Today, the museum is known as having one of the best collections of minerals and fossils in the province. In 2011, the museum grew even more when it took over the library's space.

The Princeton Museum in 1958
Princeton & District Museum & Archives

discover the ancient past

SCORPIONFLY FOSSIL

The actual fossil is about five centimetres long. That's small. It's about the length of a house key.

Kathy Simpkins donated the fossil to the museum where she worked as a director and volunteer. She has about 30 years of experience with fossils.

Now the fossil lives in the Royal BC Museum in Victoria, a museum known for its fine natural history collection. This was decided when they realized this fossil was the only one of its kind.

This species of scorpionfly is now extinct but a similar species is still living in the forests of coastal Chile, an area that, like ancient British Columbia, is known for its mild climate.

Fossils were first found in the Princeton area by George Mercer Dawson in the 1870s along the shale near the creek beds. Since then, the area has become known for several important finds.

Kathy unearthed the rare fossil while sorting through a shale pile near an old mine called Allenby, just outside Princeton.

This discovery caused a great deal of excitement in the world of fossils because of its rareness.

When this insect was alive, East Asia and North America were joined together by land.

JUST THE FACTS

ICE PLOW

WHAT IS IT? When a foot of ice was on the lake, ice men would cut strips in the ice with the ice plow. These strips would then be cut into blocks and transported to the ice house by wagon.

WHAT DOES IT LOOK LIKE? It was pulled by horses and made of steel. Picture it as about the size of a large lawnmower. The cutting teeth fit in a straight line. Each tooth was longer than the last. It was steered by plow handles along a straight line marked into the ice.

WHERE DOES IT COME FROM? Gerald Harker ran the ice harvesting business. His sons, Len and Roy, restored and donated the ice plow to the museum.

WHO USED IT? This was a tool of the ice harvesting trade. In the Princeton area, this was run by Bill Garrison, and later by Gerald Harker. A crew of 75 ice harvesters could cut 1,360,777 kilograms of ice. That's about 200 times heavier than an adult elephant.

WOULD YOU BELIEVE?

Ice from here was taken to ice houses all the way west of Spokane, Washington, by the Great Northern Railway. One year the harvest was so big, it needed 3,000 railcars to transport the ice.

CONNECTIONS

A Glaciarium Poster
S G Fairbrother (Firm).
Alexander Turnbull
Library, NZ.

In June 1844, the Glaciarium – London, England's, first artificial skating rink – opened. It was a pretty place with an alpine theme. The problem was the smell. It was terrible. Back then ice couldn't be manufactured to create a rink in the summer. So they used a mixture of pig fat and salts. The rink soon closed.

WHY IS THE ICE PLOW IMPORTANT IN THIS AREA?

This ice plow is a demonstration of how technology is always changing. When people first began gathering ice and storing it successfully, or exporting it to different countries, it was considered modern. Now we rarely think about how we keep things cold. The ice harvesters played an important role in the community and in neighbouring communities. It was a hard, physical job that might be completely forgotten if not for machines like the ice plow.

My Turn

Are you ready to paint with ice? First of all, start by checking if it's okay with the adults in your life. If it's fine, let's go.

1. Here's what you need: water, a pad of paper, a packet of food colouring, Popsicle sticks and an ice tray. Start by pouring water into the ice tray. Put a different drop of food colouring in each cube section. Experiment and create some of your own colours by mixing them. Place a Popsicle stick in each section, and place the ice tray in the freezer.

2. Once the water is frozen, take the tray out of the freezer and remove the frozen cubes by their sticks. (Remember to place something over the table you are working on to protect it.)

3. Now hold onto the stick and paint on your paper. Play with texture by warming up the ice quickly by rubbing it hard on the paper, or very slowly. Have fun!

Tell Me More

Before there was electric refrigeration, ice was big business. People all over the globe wanted ice to keep their **perishables**. Ice was exported from cold places to places where people needed to keep things cold. In the ice house, sawdust was used as insulation to keep the ice from melting, making sure it would last for many months.

From 1915 to 1925, this ice plow was used every winter to gather ice from nearby Otter Lake in Tulameen. Ice continued to be delivered to some local businesses into the 1960s. There were even some businesses that actually had small ice houses for storage.

JUST THE FACTS

WHAT IS IT? General William T. Sherman owned this sword. He played a big role in the American Civil War between 1861 and 1865. That was before Canada became an official country. In the American Civil War, the conflict was between the northern states (the Union) and the southern states (the Confederacy). The president during the war was a very famous man called Abraham Lincoln.

WHAT DOES IT LOOK LIKE? The sword is forged steel with a brass-coloured guard and black grip. It is about a metre long.

WHERE DOES IT COME FROM? The sword is on loan to the museum from the Allison family.

WHO USED IT? General William T. Sherman was an important Union military leader during the American Civil War. He carried the sword in August 1883 as he travelled from Coeur d'Alene, Idaho, through to northern Washington state into Canada at Osoyoos Lake and out toward the Similkameen. This trip was part of a Final Inspection Tour before his retirement.

Thompson/Okanagan

› PRINCETON & DISTRICT MUSEUM & ARCHIVES

CIVIL WAR SWORD

Tell Me More

While in the Similkameen, Sherman and his party camped near the Allison Ranch, close to what is now Princeton. Sherman dined with the Allison family. The family had nine children. Sherman made a big impression on them.

Sherman enjoyed playing with the children. He had them pretending to be soldiers, marching all around. One of the Allison children, Little George, was so entertaining that Sherman gave him his sword to pretend with. The boy marched proudly around with it. Allison family lore is that, before the Sherman party left the next day, the general's final act was to present the sword to them. The **scabbard** rotted away, but the sword survived.

? WOULD YOU BELIEVE?

The sword passed through the family until it eventually came into George's possession. In about 1960, after George's death, his wife Violet was in need of money, so she decided to try and sell the sword. Only she got mixed up and said the sword belonged to another famous American Civil War general, General Ulysses S. Grant. Nobody wanted to buy the sword.

Today, the sword remains in the family. It's on loan to the museum. Some years ago, an American visitor to the museum offered to purchase it, but the family declined, wanting to keep it as a family memento.

CONNECTIONS

On St. Ninian's Isle in Shetland, Scotland, on July 4, 1958, a schoolboy named Douglas Coutts discovered a treasure under the remains of a medieval church. He was helping on a dig with Professor A. C. O'Dell of Aberdeen University. The treasure was 28 silver and silver-gilt objects made during the second half of the eighth century. Unlike Little George's property, though, this treasure did not stay with Douglas. The treasure is displayed in the National Museum of Scotland in Edinburgh. A replica of the treasure is displayed at the Shetland Museum.

Images: Wikimedia Commons, Johnbod

My Turn

During the American Civil War, soldiers from both the North and South longed for news from home. Often, they reread letters from family over and over. Imagine if someone from your family was a soldier. What kind of news would you share with them? Write them a letter and see.

★ WHY IS THE CIVIL WAR SWORD IMPORTANT IN THIS AREA?

The sword links a small isolated community in British Columbia to a famous man who had a large impact on American history. It allows us a peak into the personality of a man whose army was feared during the American Civil War by the people of the South and admired by the people of the North.

General William T. Sherman
Image: Wikimedia Commons, dbking

Top left: Susan Allison **Top right:** John Fall Allison **Bottom:** Main St. Princeton c.1920
Photos: Princeton & District Museum & Archives

OLIVER & DISTRICT HERITAGE SOCIETY MUSEUM

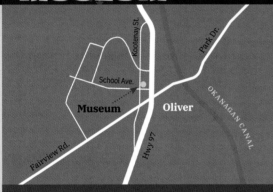

JUST THE FACTS

WHERE IS IT? 474 School Avenue, Oliver, BC, V0H 1T0; (250) 498-4027
oliverheritage.ca

ARE PHOTOGRAPHS ALLOWED? Yes, there's even a selfie room with costumes.

HOW DID IT START? The museum is the brainchild of the Oliver Heritage Society, now known as Oliver and District Heritage Society. The name was changed to include the surrounding district, area "C."

WHERE HAS IT LIVED?

At first glance, the museum looks like a quaint old-fashioned bungalow, the perfect setting for a fairy tale, but it has an unexpected history. Built in 1924, it was the second public building to be erected in Oliver, and it was made to feel like a house on purpose. Why? To support the idea of equality and show that the local government worked for the community and not the other way around. This was an important decision in a town like Oliver, where many of its villagers worked hard physical jobs on the South Okanagan Lands Project, building a new state-of-the-art irrigation system known as "The Ditch." This nickname is very popular with locals and visitors.

WHERE DO THE ITEMS COME FROM?

Most of the items here are donations.

HOW HAS IT CHANGED?

The building was a British Columbia Provincial Police (BCPP) detachment from 1924 to 1950. In 1950, around the same time as a bottle of pop cost only five cents, it was taken over by the RCMP until 1966, when the RCMP got a new building and our national broadcaster, the CBC, began airing in colour.

After the RCMP left, the building was used for residential, low-income housing. Finally, 15 years later as part of the town of Oliver's 60th anniversary celebrations, the building was given to the museum.

In a museum you can:

learn how to be an inventor

KANGAROO PLATFORM

The Kangaroo is a self-propelled, hydraulic fruit-picking platform designed by John Rotheisler in 1961. It's designed to be used by a single operator.

"Self-propelled" is just a fancy way of saying it can move on its own. Hydraulics is the use of pressurized liquids to make things move.

The different models of the orchard-picking platforms are all named after animals. There's a kangaroo, a giraffe and even a squirrel. These pictures are of the Giraffe.

This was the first Kangaroo built by Rotheisler Equipment Ltd.

This machine revolutionized the process of picking tree fruits and pruning orchards not only in the South Okanagan but across the world.

The Kangaroo's inventor, John Rotheisler, who is also from Oliver, donated it to the museum.

The Kangaroo is still used in orchards throughout the Okanagan and the world.

The size is hard to describe. Think of a medium-sized speedboat with a long ladder and a diving platform attached to it.

JUST THE FACTS

WHAT IS IT? A table from a local packing house where workers would pack apples.

WHAT DOES IT LOOK LIKE? It's about the size of a high school student's desk and designed to making packing more efficient and easier.

WHERE DOES IT COME FROM? The museum doesn't know much about how the table made it to the museum. Here's what it does know: it was donated by a local and used in an Oliver packing house. The rest is a mystery.

WHO USED IT? It was used by "The Applebox Belles," the women working in the Oliver packing houses. In the beginning of the 20th century, the number of orchards in the Okanagan expanded rapidly. To meet the need for apples across Canada, packing houses began to open in the valley. Only women were employed as apple wrappers and packers. The packers were known as Apple Wrapper Flappers.

Thompson/Okanagan
› OLIVER & DISTRICT HERITAGE SOCIETY MUSEUM

APPLE PACKING TABLE

Tell Me More

The packer faced an empty box. On the right side of the apple table there was a sorting area filled with apples. To the left of the table were wrapping papers. The wooden bench where the packer sat was on wheels and sloped to make the job easier. In front of the packer was an empty apple crate. The apples would be packed according to size and grade – Extra Fancy, Fancy and Cee grade. Once a box had been packed, the packer would wheel her bench to a nearby conveyor belt that took the boxes to the pressman. Each packer had an assigned number and would put a ticket with their number in the box. If a box wasn't packed properly, it could be sent back to the right packer.

The pressman would stamp the side of the box with the variety, grade and number of apples in the box. Packers worked hard for a living. Shifts were ten hours long, and in that time the average packer could pack anywhere from 120 to 200 50-pound boxes. The rate of pay was 3.75 cents per box. An experienced packer could make as much as $7.00 a shift.

Photo: S. Lesley Buxton

WOULD YOU BELIEVE?

In the 1940s and 1950s, apple-packing competitions were held throughout the Okanagan. The last competition was held in 1952. This was won by Oliver's own apple-packing queen, Anne Peterman, who worked at McLean & Fitzpatrick. At the time, she'd been a packer for 14 years. Anne was crowned Queen Delicious. Her prize was $500, the same as winning $5,000 today.

My Turn

We all know apples taste delicious, but did you know you can use them to make an art stamp? To do this you will need some paper, a pen, some paint, a mixing tray, a paint brush and a knife to cut the apple in half (for safety reasons, ask an adult to cut the apple in half).

After the apple is cut in half, sketch an outline of your stamp. Remember this will appear as a mirror image. Carve out the shape on the cut surface of the apple, using a spoon, plastic knife or straw. Once your carving is finished, paint the stamp. Be careful to cover it evenly. Now place the stamp on the paper. Repeat with different designs. This is a great way to make one-of-a-kind wrapping paper.

Even in ancient times the apple was a popular snack. The ancient Romans loved apples. In the winter, they created dishes using dried apples, and in the summer, they cooled down with them. The apple was so popular with Romans that whenever the army settled in an area, they planted their seeds. Some might say they are responsible for spreading apples across Europe.

OLP.992.57.2

★ WHY IS THE APPLE PACKING TABLE IMPORTANT IN THIS AREA?

During this time in Canada, it was very rare for a woman to make a good wage for paid work outside the home. This work gave Okanagan women access to a good income, allowing them the chance to feel independent and contribute to their family's incomes.

JUST THE FACTS

WHAT IS IT? This is the original Fairview Jail. It was built over a hundred years ago in a gold mining town of the same name, just west of the town of Oliver.

WHAT DOES IT LOOK LIKE? The Fairview Jail is about the height of an African elephant and about the width of three of them squished together.

WHERE DOES IT COME FROM? The jail was moved from its original site to Oliver because of repeated acts of vandalism.

WHO USED IT? It was used as Fairview's police office and lockup, with two cells for short-term detention. The main room would have housed the police constable's desk. If it had been busy, it would have felt cramped, as it's not large at all. Two of the known constables who ran the jail were Constable Fred Elkine and Constable Ron Hewitt.

All photos this spread: Oliver & District Heritage Society Museum

› OLIVER & DISTRICT HERITAGE SOCIETY MUSEUM

FAIRVIEW JAIL

Tell Me More

The town of Fairview was established about ten years before the jail was built. A prospector called One-Armed Reed and his partner Ryan discovered the first mineral deposit at the site. But, strangely, they never returned. It wasn't until later, when Fred Gwatkins and George Sheehan staked the first **claim** in 1887, that Fairview began to grow. Word quickly spread, and not long after that prospectors, dreaming they'd strike it rich, began arriving from all over the world.

Naturally, the growing population needed **amenities**, so soon businesses began to appear, including hotels, a general store, a saloon and government buildings. We don't know who built the jail. In a town filled with hard-living working men, it's probably safe to conclude some of Fairview's inhabitants sometimes drank too much. No doubt there was a great deal of loneliness, boredom and financial stress in this isolated community. The Fairview constables were most likely used to breaking up fights.

In its heyday, Fairview had five operating mines. The town's people boasted that it was "the largest city north of San Francisco." Sadly, the wealth did not last. Only 15 years later the town began to decline as the gold became less plentiful. Soon people began to move away – some to nearby Oliver. These days, we think of Fairview as a **ghost town**.

? WOULD YOU BELIEVE?

The Fairview Jail was mainly used to house drunk miners who needed a place to sleep it off, but the town has two recorded murders. It's highly likely those accused men spent some time in this jail before they were sent to prison.

My Turn

See how quickly you can say the list of slang words for jail. Try challenging your friends. Be careful. Some of these words are trickier than they seem.

★ WHY IS THE FAIRVIEW JAIL IMPORTANT IN THIS AREA?

Boom-and-bust mining towns like Fairview have a reputation for being lawless and wild. The jail was one of the two remaining buildings. Strangely, the other surviving building was the church, which is now the Okanagan Falls United Church. The jail offers us insight into the lives of people living in Fairview. On a larger scale it also serves as a warning. **Boomtowns** like Fairview often depend on a single resource like mining or logging. When this runs out, they often become abandoned quickly. This is a good reminder that our resources aren't endless.

CONNECTIONS

Hoosegow, mainline joint, skinner joint, stoney lonesome, con college, glasshouse, bucket, club fed, greybar hotel, big house, slammer, calaboose, castle, cooler, country club, crowbar hotel, digger, farm, guardhouse, hole, joint, jug, juvie, pen, pokey, rock, sneezer, stockade, the clink: What do all these words have in common? They are all slang terms for jail. Can you believe there are so many?

The Fairview Jail.

The Fairview townsite, now abandonded.

11 REVELSTOKE MUSEUM & ARCHIVES

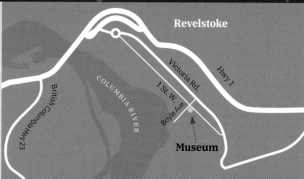

Revelstoke

Victoria Rd.

Hwy 1

1 St. W. Ave

COLUMBIA RIVER

British Columbia Hwy.

British Columbia Hwy 23

Boyle Ave.

Museum

JUST THE FACTS

WHERE IS IT? 315 1st Street West, Revelstoke, BC, V0E 2S0; (250) 837-3067
revelstokemuseum.ca

ARE PHOTOGRAPHS ALLOWED? Yes.

HOW DID IT START? The Revelstoke and District Historical Association formed in 1958. This group of people was worried that the history of the region around the town of Revelstoke could be lost. The group's goal was to research local history, to encourage others to become interested in that history and preserve historical materials in a museum where it could collect, store and display objects.

The group started collecting items in 1960. In 1963, it moved into the basement of the former public health building.

WHERE HAS IT LIVED?

The museum stayed in the basement for 11 years. Then it moved to the old post office building (built in 1926). It hasn't moved from this building, but the museum and **archives** have expanded from the basement and first floor to the whole building.

The name has also changed. The association is now called the Revelstoke Museum & Archives Association.

WHERE DO THE ITEMS COME FROM?

With very few exceptions, items in the collection have been donated. The collection focuses on items made or used in Revelstoke and in the surrounding district.

HOW HAS IT CHANGED?

One major change is how the space in the museum is used. Many partitions that divided the space have been removed, creating a bright and open feeling. Exhibits tell the stories of the community. While most exhibits will be up for three to five years, the Sinixt Nation exhibit, the Revelstoke community exhibit and the ski exhibit are permanent.

Sometimes people don't think about how spaces outside a museum change. The Heritage Garden was created in 2004 to make a downtown green space in what used to be a delivery alley next to the building. It is maintained by a group of dedicated volunteers.

In a museum you can:

learn about poisons
POISON BOTTLE

People used poisons to kill rats and other household pests

Household poisons were sold in pharmacies in the late 1800s and early 1900s

Poison bottles were made of coloured glass so they would stand out from other clear glass bottles

This bottle has raised letters and a skull and crossbones

Many people living in the 1800s and early 1900s could not read, and raised letters and symbols made poison bottles easily identified

The museum's bottle is bright blue

In the USA and Britain, pharmacies started storing poison in bottles with interesting shapes like skulls, leg bones and coffins.

JUST THE FACTS

WHAT IS IT? This is a saddle meant for carrying things, not people, on the back of a horse.

WHAT DOES IT LOOK LIKE? The saddle is made from pieces of wood and leather straps. It fits over the horse's back.

WHERE DOES IT COME FROM? The packsaddle, which was made and used in Revelstoke, was donated by Revelstoke City Hall in 1962. Unfortunately, no one knows how or why it had the saddle in the first place.

WHO USED IT? The packsaddle was used by Andrew Rupert Westerberg, who was known locally as "Ole the Bear." Ole was a nickname often given to people who came from Scandinavia, and he had many encounters with bears. Andrew was born in Sweden and came to Revelstoke in 1900. That was 15 years after the last spike was driven into the railway tracks at Craigellachie, just 50 kilometres west of Revelstoke.

When Royal Mail Canada advertised for a person to deliver mail to the Big Bend area north of Revelstoke, they hired Andrew. Think about the mail carriers you see in your neighbourhood. Maybe they walk their routes, or maybe they use a car or truck. Andrew's route was a 160-kilometre round trip, which he made 15 times a year. He used skis or snowshoes in the winter, and a pack horse in the summer. He delivered the mail on this route for 25 years.

› REVELSTOKE MUSEUM & ARCHIVES

PACKSADDLI

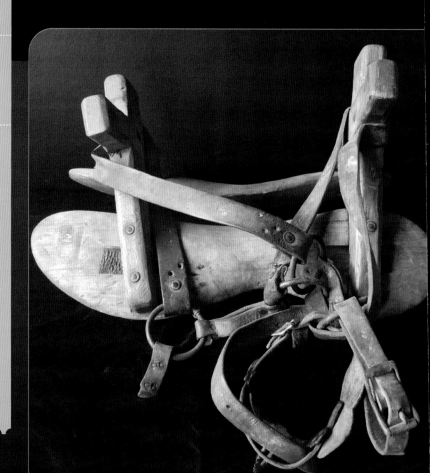

WOULD YOU BELIEVE?

Andrew once made snowshoes for a horse to lead it back to Revelstoke after a heavy snowfall in Big Bend.

My Turn

Imagine you are Andrew Rupert Westerberg. You have seen the Royal Mail Canada ad for the mail route from Revelstoke to Big Bend and you are interested in applying. What skills would you list to make sure you got the job?

CONNECTIONS

Packsaddles were designed to allow a horse to do heavy lifting and carrying. The Plains people – the many Indigenous groups who live across the prairies from the Rocky Mountains to southeastern Manitoba – came up with a different kind of carrier called the travois.

Two long poles crossed at the top of the horse's shoulders and formed what you might think of as an upside-down *V*. In the wide part, the user would place some netting or a wooden frame to carry objects. The wide ends of the upside-down *V* would skim across the prairie grass on the ground behind the horse. The travois was best suited to flat ground. It did not work well in forests or through **gorges** or ravines.

Tell Me More

A packsaddle is very different from a saddle you would use for riding. In fact, if you tried to sit on this saddle, you would be very sore quite quickly. Andrew made the saddle himself to use on his pack horses. The packsaddle probably sat on a saddle blanket to make sure the horse was comfortable and didn't get any sores from the saddle rubbing on its skin. Two long wooden slats were shaped to fit the curve of the animal's back. These ran parallel, on either side of the horse's backbone. Attached to these slats were wooden bars that crossed above the horse's spine. These crossed bars were used for hanging the sacks with mail and supplies. Of course, the saddle was attached to the horse with leather straps.

WHY IS THE PACKSADDLE IMPORTANT IN THIS AREA?

The story of "Ole the Bear" and this packsaddle emphasizes how far Revelstoke and the surrounding areas were from anywhere else, especially before cars and trucks became affordable.

Andrew Rupert Westerberg, known locally as "Ole the Bear" on his Big Bend mail run, c.1920.

Photo: Revelstoke Museum & Archives

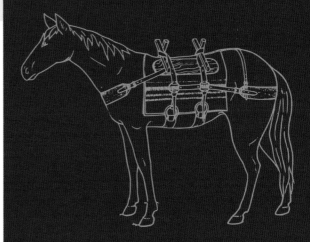

JUST THE FACTS

WHAT IS IT? A fur press was used to squish all the furs together to make them into a bale or bundle that was easily transported.

WHAT DOES IT LOOK LIKE? The fur press is huge. It's 248 centimetres tall, about the height of your bedroom. It's 163 centimetres wide – about the width of two stoves sitting side by side – and as deep as a refrigerator (81.28 centimetres). It is constructed from wood.

WHERE DOES IT COME FROM? Local builders made the press in around 1911. It was used by Francis Beddoes (also known as F. B.) Wells in his store on Front Street in Revelstoke. The fur press was donated in 1974 by F. B.'s son, Frank Wells. Frank operated the store for several years after his father died.

WHO USED IT? When F. B. first came to Revelstoke in 1886, he worked for the Canadian Pacific Railway, but three years later, he opened a menswear store on Front Street. His business slogan was "Wells Wear Wears Well."

F. B. also bought furs from local trappers and sold them to furriers in Winnipeg, Montreal and other places. That's why he needed a fur press.

Tell Me More

To make a bundle of furs, a piece of canvas was laid on the floor of the press. The furs were piled on the canvas. A rectangular plate was screwed down to press the furs and make them more compact for shipping. The furs were made into a bundle called a bale.

› REVELSTOKE MUSEUM & ARCHIVES

FUR PRESS

Fred Robinson, Charles Skene Durrand with their furs, circa 1 Bunty Skene is peeking out beh the furs

WOULD YOU BELIEVE?

*You can still see some of the dates and the numbers of certain furs F. B. bought. The museum has **ledgers** of the sales F. B. made. But you can also see some of these records handwritten on the side of the fur press.*

CONNECTIONS

North America was not the only place where furs could be found. Around the same time as Jacques Cartier arrived in Canada, Russians were getting furs from Siberia, an area they had conquered. The Siberian natives were very good hunters and trappers and could remove the skins from animals without damaging them. While they didn't use a fur press like F. B. Wells, they did press furs between two boards to transport them down rivers. Rivers were like roads between the hunting and trapping grounds and the central trading areas. Because the boards were made of wood, these presses were called "timbers."

A Siberian sable depicted on a Russian stamp

Image: Wikimedia Commons, designer Yury Artsimenev

Siberian fur trader at the fair in Leipzig, Germany (c. 1800)

Image: Wikimedia Commons, author unknown

My Turn

Why do you think Wells's slogan, "Wells Wear Wears Well" is a good one? How is an old-fashioned printing press like a fur press?

⭐ WHY IS THE FUR PRESS IMPORTANT IN THIS AREA?

F. B. was a pioneer entrepreneur in Revelstoke. That means he set up a business that most other people may not have thought of, or tried. The fur trade that brought the Hudson's Bay Company and other trading companies and settlers to North America from the 1600s was over by the 1900s. So why did F. B. have a fur press built for his store in 1911?

F. B. knew people were still buying and selling furs. He also knew that trappers kept the location of their traplines as secret as miners kept the location of their mining **claims**. In fact, many miners also had traplines and usually made more money from trapping than from mining.

The museum has records from F. B. Wells's business. In April of 1914, one trapper was paid more than $600 for about 100 marten furs. This would have been equivalent to what an average person would make in six months.

Fox, coyote, rabbit, marten, and beaver are all hunted for their fur.

GREENWOOD MUSEUM & VISITOR CENTRE

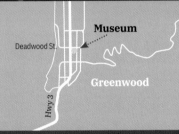

Museum

Deadwood St.

Greenwood

Hwy 3

JUST THE FACTS

WHERE IS IT? 214 South Copper Avenue, Greenwood, BC, V0H 1J0; (250) 445-6355
greenwoodmuseum.com

ARE PHOTOGRAPHS ALLOWED? Yes.

HOW DID IT START? The museum was started by the Greenwood Museum Association, later renamed the Greenwood Heritage Society, which wanted to preserve the stories of this historic city. Today, Greenwood is the smallest city in Canada, but during the late 1890s it was a boomtown. Usually boomtowns start because an important resource, like gold, is found in the area. In Greenwood, they discovered copper. Often boomtowns disappear as soon as that resource is gone.

WHERE HAS IT LIVED?

In 1967, the city gave the organization a space in the town's courthouse where council chambers are now. Today, visitors can tour the historic courthouse that was built in 1902 – 1903. The courthouse is famed for its beauty and seven-metre-high ceiling. Before the space was a museum, it was used as a place for the RCMP to live.

In 1982, the museum moved to Copper Avenue where it remains today. The museum is completely run by volunteers. There are no paid staff. It's open to the public from May 1 to October 31. The museum holds an afternoon tea each year to raise money for the museum. During the winter, museum volunteers are kept busy with correspondence, helping researchers, ongoing improvements to the exhibits and cleaning.

WHERE DO THE ITEMS COME FROM?

The museum relies on donations.

HOW HAS IT CHANGED?

The museum hopes that one day it will be able to employ a full-time curator.

learn how people entertained themselves in the past

COLIN "SCOTT" MCRAE'S VIOLIN

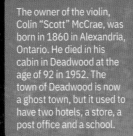

The owner of the violin, Colin "Scott" McCrae, was born in 1860 in Alexandria, Ontario. He died in his cabin in Deadwood at the age of 92 in 1952. The town of Deadwood is now a ghost town, but it used to have two hotels, a store, a post office and a school.

Scott loved music. He played the violin, the mouth organ and the chanter (which looks like a recorder with finger holes).

The violin and Canada have a long history. The first record of one being played here was in 1645.

A violin and a fiddle are the same instrument. Both have four strings, and they are both played with a bow. It's the style of music played on the instrument that makes the big difference.

When we think of a violin, we think of classical music and chamber music. Lots of different kinds of music are played on fiddles, like country, folk and Cajun.

Not only was Scott a musician, he was also a prospector, a government land surveyor, a trapper, a taxidermist, a historian and a member of the Pioneer Society.

McRae Creek rest area, on the Crowsnest Highway, not far from Christina Lake, is named after Scott.

Doreen MacLean, the museum's president, inherited Scott's dog after Scott died. Her father had known Scott since he was young. The dog, Jim, was Doreen's first pet. She was 3 or 4 when she inherited him. She remembers he used to follow her to school.

JUST THE FACTS

WHAT IS IT? This small room looks like one used by a Japanese Canadian family during their internment in Greenwood.

WHAT DOES IT LOOK LIKE? The room is about 6.5 square metres in size and is dominated by a wooden bunk bed with well-used bedding. (The British Columbia Security Commission issued the blankets.) There's a small side table for keeping the family's tea, cups and teapot, as well as a long, low, narrow table against the wall for keeping their pots and other cooking implements. There is just about enough space for an adult to stand between the bed and wall. There is very little space to dress.

WHERE DOES IT COME FROM? The Japanese family room was added to the museum in 1998 by a group of museum volunteers. The small rustic room was typical of the living quarters these families had to endure during the internment years. In later years, the museum's volunteers added the four children in the bed and the one child standing by his mother. Over the years donated artifacts were added. Communal living was the norm during these times. There was a stove in the centre of each storey, where each family took turns to cook.

WHO USED IT? The residents were mostly women, children and the elderly. Healthy men were put to work in labour camps away from their families. Can you imagine what it would be like in a twin-size bed with all your siblings? Some families with lots of kids lay sideways across the bed in order to make more room.

› GREENWOOD MUSEUM & VISITOR CENTRE

REPLICA OF ROOM USED BY A JAPANESE CANADIAN FAMILY DURING THEIR INTERNMENT

Tell Me More

During the Second World War, when Canada was at war with Japan, 1,200 Japanese Canadians were interned in Greenwood. The Japanese Canadians were not trusted by the Canadian government and seen as the enemy, even though some of the men had fought for Canada in the Great War (First World War). The Canadian government was able to send Japanese Canadians to internment camps because of the **War Measures Act**. This act gave the government extra powers during wartime.

Greenwood was the first internment site in BC. Before the Japanese Canadians arrived, there were only 200 people living in Greenwood, and it was in danger of becoming a ghost town. Empty old buildings like the Armstrong Hotel and the Gulley Block were portioned off into small rooms where families could eat and sleep. Each landing of the building had a large kitchen with a wood-burning stove. Most floors had between 15 to 20 families sharing the kitchen and bathroom. Imagine how long you m have had to wait for the bathroom!

Conditions were very cramped and busy with so many people sharing. There were all sorts of problems: cockroaches, fire hazards and froze pipes because of cold winter days.

In the beginning, some of the townspeople resented the newcom but this soon changed once they go to know the new residents. The tow began to thrive with more people to work, and the town's shopkeepers loved having more customers. Seve sawmills opened, benefitting from the new workforce. However, we mustn't forget that, although the tov benefitted from having more people the Japanese Canadians interned in Greenwood had lost businesses and homes and their entire way of life on the coast. They could not go back, a the Canadian government did not gi them back their possessions.

WOULD YOU BELIEVE?

In 1988, Prime Minster Brian Mulroney apologized to the Japanese Canadians who were interned during the war and awarded them financial compensation. Compensation means to give someone money to try and make up a hardship – this could be physical, or emotional, or both.

My Turn

How do you think the Japanese Canadian kids entertained themselves when they were interned? Do some research and learn about a Japanese game that doesn't involve a screen of any kind.

CONNECTIONS

In the United States, during the Second World War, Japanese Americans were also forced to move into internment camps. Sixty-two percent of the internees were United States citizens. In Canada, the majority of internees were Canadian by birth.

Japanese girls in Greenwood
Photo: Greenwood Museum

⭐ WHY IS THE ROOM IMPORTANT IN THIS AREA?

Looking at this room, we are reminded of a time in Canadian history when our government acted with prejudice, but we are also reminded of people who stood up to that racism. In 1945, when the war ended, the

Dinner for Japanese internees
Photo: Greenwood Museum

BC government did not wish the Japanese Canadians to return to the coast. They were told to "Go east of the Rockies or repatriate to Japan." The Greenwood Board of Trade said this was unfair. This was unusual since most communities agreed with the government's idea. In Greenwood, the Japanese Canadians were told they could stay. In 1949, there were still about 700 Japanese Canadians there.

JUST THE FACTS

› GREENWOOD MUSEUM & VISITOR CENTRE

PORCELAIN SCULPTURE OF THE THREE GRACES

WHAT IS IT? This sculpture portrays the Three Graces, characters from Greek mythology. It's about 23 centimetres tall and made of white porcelain.

WHAT DOES IT LOOK LIKE? The Three Graces are naked. They stand with their arms around each other. It looks as if they are telling each other secrets. The centre head is broken off. The donor of the piece said it's been like that for a long time. Inside of the sculpture there appears to be pine needles or hay.

WHERE DOES IT COME FROM? The note left by the anonymous donor explained that his or her great-grandfather's brother had "apparently" removed the sculpture from a tombstone in Phoenix, BC (a mining town not far from Greenwood). The donor's great-grandfather and great-uncle both lived there.

   The donor didn't know if the sculpture was removed shortly after they left the town in the early 1920s, or on a visit afterwards. Both the donor's great-grandfather and great-uncle died in the late '40s. The donor also said they couldn't imagine something so fragile and hollow being placed on a tombstone, but if it was, it certainly belonged at the museum.

   Try and picture the donor's great-uncle grabbing the sculpture on his way out of town as a keepsake. Perhaps he knew the person whose gravestone it belonged to, or maybe he just took it impulsively and regretted it for years. The sculpture has a decidedly feminine feel. Perhaps it even belonged to a woman the uncle had been in love with.

WHO USED IT? This piece arrived mysteriously at the museum one year around Christmas. There was no return address on the box, but there was a typewritten note.

WOULD YOU BELIEVE?

Today, Phoenix is a ghost town, but during its peak, when the copper mine was active, it was a booming town with an opera house, a hockey

The city of Phoenix

team, a ballroom, its own stagecoach line and a banquet hall. When the town went bust in 1920, many of its inhabitants simply left their homes and belongings. Later, workers were hired to come and clear away the town; churches, stores, halls, the hospital and even the skating rink were all taken to be used by other communities. Today, the only remaining parts of the town are the First World War **cenotaph** *and the pioneer cemetery.*

The Cenotaph at Phoenix

Photo: Wikimedia Commons, Violetsteel777

Tell Me More

The Three Graces are the daughters of Zeus (the ruler of the Greek gods) and an Oceanid (a water nymph) named Eurynome. Their names are Aglaia meaning brightness, Euphrosyne meaning joyfulness and Thalia meaning bloom. They are said to represent beauty, charm and grace.

The Three Graces waited on Aphrodite, the goddess of love. It was their duty to grant young women gifts of beauty, charm and goodness. They were also supposed to spread a feeling of goodness around. The Three Graces were linked to the Nine Muses, who were closely associated with music and the arts.

My Turn

Imagine you had to leave your home in a hurry. If you could take only one thing with you, what would it be and why?

CONNECTIONS

In a famous museum in London, England, called the V&A (Victoria and Albert), there is a sculpture of *The Three Graces* in white marble by an Italian artist called Antonio Canova. This artist was once the most celebrated in Europe. One of his biggest fans was Napoleon Bonaparte. Napoleon Bonaparte was a French emperor who tried to conquer Europe. Canova did several sculptures of him.

In the V&A's gift shop, visitors can buy a patch for their jeans featuring an updated version of the Three Graces by Scratchy Patchy using images of supermodels.

⭐ WHY IS THE SCULPTURE IMPORTANT IN THIS AREA?

It's an important link to BC's largest ghost town and demonstrates the human side of a boom-and-bust town. It shows that, even in this working-class town where life was tough and people worked hard, people still took time to appreciate beauty.

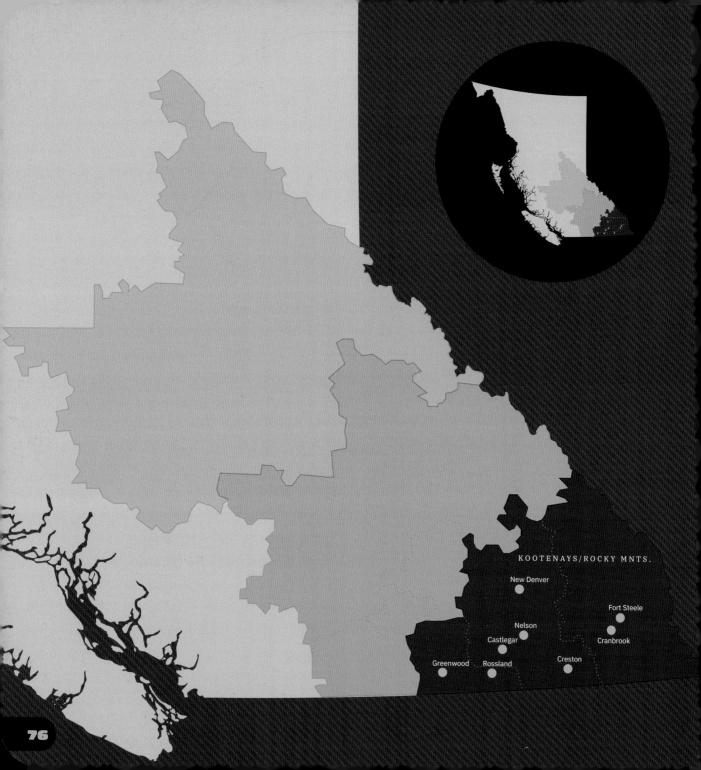

KOOTENAYS/ROCKY MNTS.

New Denver

Fort Steele

Nelson

Cranbrook

Castlegar

Creston

Greenwood   Rossland

KOOTENAY/ ROCKY MOUNTAINS

TRADITIONAL AND UNCEDED TERRITORY OF THE FOLLOWING FIRST NATIONS:

Ɂaq'am

Ktunaxa

Secwepemc

Sinixt

syilx/Okanagan

Yaqan Nukiy (Lower Kootenay)

[Insert "Map of Cranbrook Area with Activities"]

CRANBROOK HISTORY CENTRE

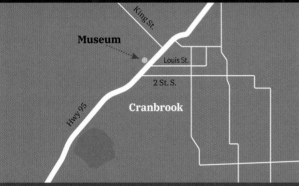

Museum
King St.
Louis St.
2 St. S.
Cranbrook
Hwy 95

JUST THE FACTS

WHERE IS IT? 57 Van Horne Street South, Box 400, Cranbrook, BC, V1C 4H9; (250) 489-3918
cranbrookhistorycentre.com

ARE PHOTOGRAPHS ALLOWED? Yes.

HOW DID IT START? The Cranbrook Archives, Museum and Landmark Foundation was founded in 1976. The museum has had three names: The Cranbrook Railway Museum, the Canadian Museum of Rail Travel and the Cranbrook History Centre.

WHERE HAS IT LIVED?

The museum originally lived two blocks from its current home. In 1987, the CPR donated the Elko Train Station, built in 1900, to the museum. If the museum hadn't taken the building, it would have been destroyed. The station was moved on a flatbed truck 40 kilometres from Elko to Cranbrook. It took three nights to move it because the movers had to lift every power and telephone line that stretched across the highway.

By 2004, the Railway Museum had outgrown its home at the Elko station and moved to its present location. It was renamed the Canadian Museum of Rail Travel.

WHERE DO THE ITEMS COME FROM?

Items have been purchased, as well as donated.

HOW HAS IT CHANGED?

The Cranbrook archives, a gift shop and a model railway have been added to the museum. One of the largest additions was the Royal Alexandra Hall. The Royal Alexandra was a luxury hotel built in the early 1900s by the Canadian Pacific Railway. The hall was the only part of Winnipeg's Royal Alexandra Hotel to be preserved. It was taken apart piece by piece and stored for 25 years until the Cranbrook History Centre bought it in 1999. It took five more years to restore.

Another important change to the museum was the construction of the train shed to protect the heritage railcars from rain, snow and sun.

Since 2015, the museum has included more local history. The museum has an ongoing partnership with the Ktunaxa First Nation and has added a new paleontology gallery and the Cranbrook history galleries.

Look at surgical instruments used in the early 1900s

SURGICAL KIT

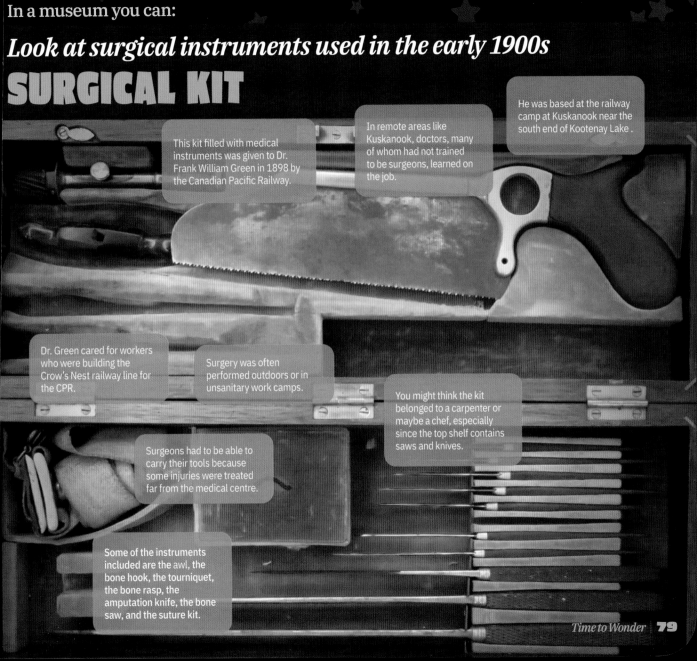

This kit filled with medical instruments was given to Dr. Frank William Green in 1898 by the Canadian Pacific Railway.

In remote areas like Kuskanook, doctors, many of whom had not trained to be surgeons, learned on the job.

He was based at the railway camp at Kuskanook near the south end of Kootenay Lake .

Dr. Green cared for workers who were building the Crow's Nest railway line for the CPR.

Surgery was often performed outdoors or in unsanitary work camps.

You might think the kit belonged to a carpenter or maybe a chef, especially since the top shelf contains saws and knives.

Surgeons had to be able to carry their tools because some injuries were treated far from the medical centre.

Some of the instruments included are the awl, the bone hook, the tourniquet, the bone rasp, the amputation knife, the bone saw, and the suture kit.

JUST THE FACTS

STUFFED TOY PANDA BEAR

WHAT IS IT? It is a child's stuffed panda bear.

WHAT DOES IT LOOK LIKE? This bear is 60 centimetres long. Its body and face are white, but it has very dark circles around its eyes and very dark ears. Its legs and arms are the same colour as its ears. The paws are white.

WHERE DOES IT COME FROM? Sometimes museums don't know where an object comes from. This doesn't make the object less important. The origin of this bear is unknown. It may have belonged to a passenger who rode the train before 1934.

WHO USED IT? Although there's no history for this bear, it probably was owned by a child. It certainly looks well loved. But there could be many other reasons the bear showed up in a train car.

Tell Me More

The panda bear now lives in one of the restored staterooms of the Curzon train car. This end car was part of the Soo-Spokane Train Deluxe passenger service, which ran from Minneapolis, Minnesota, to Spokane, Washington. So where is the Canadian connection to this train car? The train came through Canada, stopping in Moose Jaw, Medicine Hat, Fernie and right here in Cranbrook. It took three and a half days to make the trip. The Curzon had many purposes. It is described as a sleeper-buffet-library-observation car. With so many reasons to visit this car, a person could easily forget their favourite bear by accident.

WOULD YOU BELIEVE?

The family who bought the Curzon from the CPR in 1934 found this stuffed bear in an upper berth. The train car was used as a cottage on a lake in Wisconsin until 1992.

My Turn

Make up a story about the person who left this bear on the train. Where were they coming from? Where were they going? Why was the bear important to the person? Could there be a story about the person trying to find the bear?

CONNECTIONS

Stuffed toys have a very long history. The first ones to look like the modern stuffed toys we see in stores today were made by Margarete Steiff, who lived in Germany. When Margarete was 18 months old, she got polio. Her legs were paralyzed, and it was painful for her to move her right hand. She didn't let that hold her back, though. Her siblings or neighbours took her to school in a handcart (a little like a wheelbarrow). Among the subjects she studied was sewing. By 17, she qualified as a seamstress and worked with her two sisters in their dressmaker's shop.

When her sisters closed their shop, Margarete started her own clothing business. She saw a little fabric elephant in a magazine and decided to make a felt pincushion shaped like an elephant. While some people bought the pincushions for holding their pins while they sewed, others bought them as toys for their children. In six years, she sold over 5,000 stuffed elephants. She also started making other stuffed animals.

Her nephew came up with the idea of making a bear with movable arms and legs. They presented the bear at a toy fair in 1903. An American man ordered 3,000 of them. Children in the United States loved the bear. In 1906, this popular toy was given the name "teddy bear" after Theodore (Teddy) Roosevelt, the president of the United States.

★ WHY IS THE STUFFED BEAR IMPORTANT IN THIS AREA?

This bear tells us something about train travel in western Canada. Trains were not just for transporting products like wood, fruit and ore across the country. Train travel was popular with business people, workers who were travelling to find jobs and with families. This was especially true before the car became popular and affordable.

A 1913 Advertisement for Steiff products
Public Domain: Margarete Steiff GmbH

JUST THE FACTS

TRILOBITE

WHAT IS IT? About 500 million years ago, this trilobite (whose scientific name is Orygmaspis spinula) was likely a bottom feeder in an ancient ocean that covered the East Kootenay. Remember British Columbia looked very different then. Much of it was underwater. Trilobites were the first creatures on Earth that had eyes that could see. Their eyes had lenses made of rock crystal.

WHAT DOES IT LOOK LIKE? A trilobite is an invertebrate, which means it has no spine. This trilobite is oval-shaped, about four centimetres long.

WHERE DOES IT COME FROM? Chris Jenkins, an amateur paleontologist, donated this trilobite to the Cranbrook History Centre. He found the specimen in the Bull River Valley near Cranbrook.

WHO USED IT? Scientists and geologists study trilobites because these ancient species can tell us many things about prehistory and about modern times. For example, from studying trilobites, scientists can gather information about extinction, the movement of continents, biodiversity and climate change.

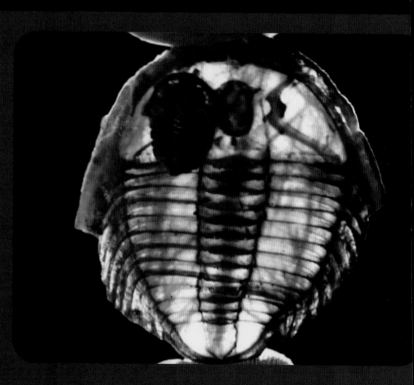

Tell Me More

Trilobites belong to the phylum Arthropoda. Some arthropods you might know are crabs, crayfish and lobsters. Arthropods' bodies have three parts, their limbs have joints (much like ours) and they have an exoskeleton – kind of like armour you see on warriors from the past.

Trilobites like this one in the museum crawled along the sea floors for about 270 million years before they were wiped out. Over 20,000 different species of trilobites have been identified. For hundreds of millions of years, they were the most successful animal on our planet. They still are – in the form of their **descendants**, insects and spiders.

Another amazing fact about trilobites is they are found on every continent on Earth, including Antarctica.

Images: Cranbrook History Centre unless otherwise specified

WOULD YOU BELIEVE?

Chris Jenkins and his friend Chris New didn't have much experience hunting for trilobites, but during their explorations in the mountains and valleys around Cranbrook they stumbled on a fossil site. Jenkins says it was "a gigantic new fossil site with trilobites laying around everywhere like Aladdin's cave." *They found several new trilobite species that attracted the attention of one of the world's top paleontologists, Dr. Brian Chatterton from the University of Alberta. They have found over 60 species of trilobites, most of which are new to science. They even have a couple of species named after them, one of which has the Latin name* Orygmaspis jenkinsi, *named after Chris Jenkins.*

CONNECTIONS

Trilobites are found worldwide. There are some really weird trilobites out there. In Russia, one had eyes that

Asaphus kowalewskii
Russian Trilobite
image: fossilmuseum.net

sat on top of five-centimetre-long stalks growing out of its head (also called the cephalon). A trilobite found in Morocco had a three-pronged, fork-shaped horn sticking out of the front of its head. The front of one trilobite found in Pennsylvania looked like the cowcatcher on an old-fashioned steam train. The largest trilobite was found in Portugal.

My Turn

In a cave in France, archaeologists found a 400-million-year-old trilobite with a hole drilled through its tail. One explanation is that ancient people in this area may have worn them as amulets or good luck charms. The Ute First Nation wore 500-million-year-old *Elrathia kingi* around their necks to keep them safe from evil spirits. Why do you think a trilobite would make a great good luck charm?

WHY IS THE TRILOBITE IMPORTANT IN THIS AREA?

We know trilobites lived at the bottom of the sea. So, if trilobites are found in an area like the East Kootenay, we know that area was under the sea. In fact, back then our continent was much further south than it is now, and most of British Columbia was under a tropical ocean.

According to the scientific theory of plate tectonics, Earth's outer shell is divided into plates. These plates shift even today, causing earthquakes

Diorama of a Silurian seafloor - homalonotid trilobite, dalmanitid trilobite at the Cleveland Museum of Natural History in Cleveland, Ohio.
Wikedia Commons: James St. John

in many parts of the world. The movement of Earth's plates millions of years ago pushed up the bottom of the sea and formed the Rocky Mountains. That's why we can find trilobites in the mountains in this area.

14 FORT STEELE HERITAGE TOWN

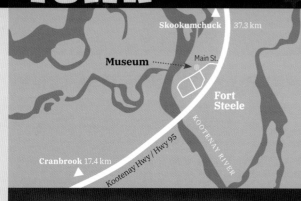

Skookumchuck 37.3 km

Museum ·······▶ Main St.

Fort Steele

KOOTENAY RIVER

Cranbrook 17.4 km

Kootenay Hwy / Hwy 95

JUST THE FACTS

WHERE IS IT? 9851 BC-95, Fort Steele, BC, V0B 1N0; (250) 417-6000
fortsteele.ca

ARE PHOTOGRAPHS ALLOWED? Yes.

HOW DID IT START? When the Canadian Pacific Railway decided to take its tracks through Cranbrook, not Fort Steele, the town suffered. The railway created jobs, and people moved to Cranbrook to find work. Then, in 1904, the provincial government offices moved to Cranbrook. That took more people away from the town. In the late 1950s, local residents wanted to bring life back to Fort Steele and asked the provincial government to protect the town. In 1961, the government declared Fort Steele a historic park.

WHERE HAS IT LIVED?

Fort Steele, once called Galbraith's Ferry, hasn't moved. The town was renamed after Superintendent Samuel B. Steele of the North West Mounted Police (NWMP). As settlers arrived, stress mounted between them and the Ktunaxa First Nation who had lived in the area for thousands of years.

In 1887, Constable Harry Anderson of the British Columbia Provincial Police arrested two young Ktunaxa men for a three-year-old murder of two miners. Chief Isadore and 25 of his men broke them out of jail.

Superintendent Steele and 75 members of the North West Mounted Police were sent to try to find solutions to the increasing tensions. After dismissing the criminal charges against the two Ktunaxa men and mediating the land problems, Steele and the NWMP left in 1888.

WHERE DO THE ITEMS COME FROM?

Most of the historic artifacts are donated. Some of the objects were things owners left behind.

HOW HAS IT CHANGED?

Some of the buildings are original. Others have been built specifically for the heritage town.

In the 1960s, the new highway split the town in half. To keep the heritage town all on one side of the highway, original buildings that were cut off by the highway were moved.

Over 98 historical buildings have been restored or reconstructed. The Wasa Hotel Museum, a replica of the original 1894 Wasa Hotel, has recently been renovated.

In a museum you can:

learn how trains were used by the logging industry

THE HERB HAWKINS LOCOMOTIVE #1077

The Herb Hawkins, built in 1923, is a full-sized locomotive engine.

This engine has belonged to six different logging companies.

It weighs about 82 metric tonnes – about the same as 200 grand pianos.

Logging railways were built from the place where logs were cut to a mill or to a river where the logs were floated down to the mill.

These railways did not carry passengers or goods – just logs and anything else needed by the logging company.

The Herb Hawkins #1077 may be the only one of its kind to have been in active service ever since it was built.

Locomotive #1077 starred in the movie Shanghai Knights with Jackie Chan and Owen Wilson.

JUST THE FACTS

TREPHINE SURGICAL TOOL

WHAT IS IT? The trephine, or trepanning instrument, is a medical instrument used to drill holes in human skulls.

WHAT DOES IT LOOK LIKE? Think of an uppercase or capital letter C, with one stroke sticking straight up from the top right and one sticking straight down from the bottom right. That's what this drill looks like. It's about 23 centimetres long, including the drill bit or burr.

WHERE DOES IT COME FROM? Fort Steele Heritage Town is not sure where this medical instrument came from.

WHO USED IT? It may have been used by Doctor Hugh Watt, who was the doctor at Fort Steele in the late 1800s.

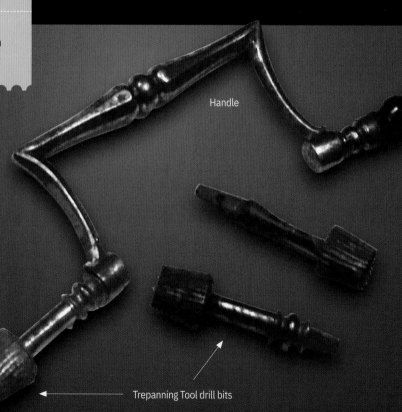

Handle

Trepanning Tool drill bits

WOULD YOU BELIEVE?

Ancient civilizations weren't lucky enough to have tools like the trepanning instrument in this museum. Very early on, they used flints (sharp pieces of stone), mussel shells, obsidian (volcanic glass) and knives. Later, they used hammers and chisels.

Between the 14th and 16th centuries CE, the Incans performed many trepanning operations. Surprisingly, even though they didn't have anesthetic or sterilization, 70 percent of people who had the operation survived. Archaeologists who examined over 800 human skulls that had been trepanned discovered this information.

Tell Me More

Sometimes when someone gets a big knock on the head, there is some bleeding inside the skull. This bleeding can put pressure on the brain, which can be dangerous. A doctor could use the trepanning instrument to drill a neat hole in the skull and let the pressure off the brain.

Around the mid-1800s, just about the time of Confederation, Canadian doctors started using ether and chloroform to put patients to sleep during operations, but before that, patients were given alcohol or herbs that would reduce the pain but not put them to sleep. Imagine what it must have been like to have a hole drilled in your head while you were still awake!

In the early 1800s, when the trepanning instrument might have been used, doctors didn't know how to fight infections. When you cut your finger, you are probably told to wash your hands with soap. Someone might also put an antiseptic cream on the cut to keep out infection. Antiseptics were not discovered until 1867, the year of Confederation. Before then patients often died of infections after an operation like trepanning.

My Turn

What can you discover about other early medical practices? Can you find other medical instruments in the museums you are visiting? What were they used for?

CONNECTIONS

Trepanning is a very old technique. As early as 7000 BCE our ancestors were performing this procedure. There is evidence it was practised by the Romans, Chinese, Greeks, Polynesians, Africans, Mayans, Aztecs and Incas. Some cultures believed trepanning was a way to let out evil spirits.

The perimeter of the hole in this trepanated Neolithic skull is rounded off by ingrowth of new bony tissue, indicating that the patient survived the operation.

Musée cantonal d'archéologie et d'histoire de Lausanne www.mcah.ch

Wikimedia Commons, Rama

⭐ WHY IS THE TREPHINE IMPORTANT IN THIS AREA?

This instrument helps visitors understand some of the medical procedures and tools used in the early Canada. It may look like an instrument of torture, not of healing, but it is important to know that trepanation is still used today. It is used on some people to treat bleeding on the brain. However, today, if a surgeon creates a hole in a person's skull, he or she will make sure the patient is asleep, replace the bone and patch it up and treat the wound with antiseptic.

JUST THE FACTS

WHAT IS IT? A sidesaddle was designed so that the rider sat with both legs on one side of the horse. When riders use a regular saddle, they sit astride the horse. That means they have one leg on either side of the horse.

WHAT DOES IT LOOK LIKE? The sidesaddle is a leather saddle with two horns, or pommels, on the left side. There is only one stirrup, unlike the more common style of saddle that has two stirrups.

WHERE DOES IT COME FROM? The sidesaddle was bought by Mrs. Sarah Larue Galbraith, one of the first female settlers in the Kootenay. When she and her husband moved to Victoria, BC, she gave the saddle to Lucy Ban Quan, who donated it to Fort Steele in the 1990s.

WHO USED IT? Sidesaddles were used mostly by women. Sarah Galbraith met her husband, John, in Walla Walla, Washington, and after they married, she rode 650 kilometres on horseback to her new home at Galbraith's Ferry. She was a very good rider. It's hard to know if she rode using a saddle like this one, or if she rode astride the horse as most women ride today.

Mrs. Galbraith was known for her horse-riding skill. She earned the nickname "Stud Horse Sal" because she rode a very large stallion. In letters to friends and family, she talks about the adventures she would have riding alongside people from the Ktunaxa First Nation in the woods around the area.

SIDESADDLE

Photo: Fort Steele Heritage Town

Tell Me More

When riding a sidesaddle, the woman has both her legs on the left side of the horse. The saddle has two knobs called pommels or horns. The rider hooks her right leg around the pommel, which curves up, so her thigh is lying across the top centre of the saddle. There is no stirrup for her right foot. Her left foot fits into a stirrup and her left thigh fits underneath the second pommel so her leg is held in place.

WOULD YOU BELIEVE?

Esther Stace, an Australian woman who rode sidesaddle, loved to jump horses. In 1915, when Esther was 44, she set a record for jumping sidesaddle that was not broken until 2013. She and her horse Emu Plains cleared 1.98 metres at the Sydney (Australia) Royal Easter Show.

It took almost 100 years for an Irish sidesaddle rider, Susan Oakes, to break Esther's record. In 2013, Susan jumped 2.03 metres.

Mrs. Esther Stace, from Yarrowitch, riding sidesaddle and clearing a record 6'6" at the Sydney Royal Show.

WHY IS THE SIDESADDLE IMPORTANT IN THIS AREA?

Before the automobile, horses were used for transportation. Sitting astride a horse was a little awkward back then because most women wore long skirts, not pants. It was also thought to be "unladylike" for women to sit astride a horse (although many women did). The sidesaddle allowed a woman to keep both legs on one side of the horse, which was more "ladylike." This saddle tells us how men and women riders were treated differently in the early years in Canada.

My Turn

Why do you think women were encouraged to ride sidesaddle, but men weren't?

CONNECTIONS

In Europe, in the late 1300s, when there were knights in armour and jousting contests, a saddle was designed so that women sat sideways on the horse with their feet on a platform. Women often used these sidesaddles when riding as a passenger behind men. However, women wanting to ride independently also used them. They were not very stable, and women could not ride quickly. Not all women used a sidesaddle. Many sat astride their horse, just like today.

A painted "illumination" from the *Manuscrit Beuve de Hantone* showing women riding sidesaddle.
Bibliothèque nationale de France

THE CRESTON MUSEUM AND ARCHIVES

JUST THE FACTS

WHERE IS IT? 219 Devon Street, Creston, BC, V0B 1G3; (250) 428-9262
crestonmuseum.ca

ARE PHOTOGRAPHS ALLOWED? Yes, unless there is a sign that says otherwise.

HOW DID IT START? Volunteers play an important part in a museum. The Creston Museum was started by a group of volunteers who formed a historical society. At first, the society gave talks and took people on tours to local historic sites. Then, in 1979, a museum in nearby Yahk closed and wanted to sell its collection at an auction. Can you imagine? Evidence of Creston's history would have been scattered all over the world. The historical society stopped the auction and bought the collection.

WHERE HAS IT LIVED?

The museum hasn't moved, but the items have. They moved from the museum in Yahk to an old potato shed west of Creston, to an open shed in Canyon before the current building was ready.

The museum was once a house built by Rudolf Schultz. He was a master stonemason who was born in Russia. In 1952, he came to live in Creston. He spent the next 15 years constructing buildings around town and working on the house you see here. He intended to build a castle. The walls are 30 to 45 centimetres thick. The ceiling is concrete reinforced with railway tracks. Schultz never built his castle. He kept expanding the size of the house, but only on one storey.

The museum opened on September 12, 1982.

WHERE DO THE ITEMS COME FROM?

The museum at least one donation every week. A person might donate just one item, like a photograph or a whole box full of objects. Sometimes people offer the museum a house full of things. The museum purchases a few objects that might be necessary to complete an exhibit. Sometimes the staff or volunteers build something for the museum.

HOW HAS IT CHANGED?

There were only two buildings when the historical society bought the property. Now there are 11. All the buildings contain exhibits. Some exhibits are permanent, but even these change over time. Museum staff are always adjusting displays as they discover new information and receive objects that will improve the display.

In a museum you can:

learn how personal computers have changed

TRS-80 MODEL III COMPUTER

This early personal computer dates back to 1982.

In the 1980s, information was stored on removable, five-inch, thin, flexible, magnetic disks. This computer had two disk drives that could store 360KB of data.

It weighs 20 kilograms and would have taken up all the space on your desk.

It was the first computer the local newspaper, the *Creston Valley Advance,* ever bought.

It came with 64KB of random access memory (RAM). One gigabyte of RAM is equal to one million KB.

Before computers, reporters wrote their stories using typewriters. They couldn't move sentences or paragraphs using "cut" and "paste."

The TRS-80 Model III used only one electrical outlet. The Model I needed five!

Photo: Wikimedia Commons, Bilby

JUST THE FACTS

WHAT IS IT? The logging arch was invented before motorized vehicles like trucks and tractors. It made it easier to move large logs to the mill over very bumpy roads.

WHAT DOES IT LOOK LIKE? The wheels, which are the main part of the logging arch, are over three metres in diameter. That's the height of an average one-storey house. Each wheel weighs about 363 kilograms. A tow bar attached to a team of horses.

WHERE DOES IT COME FROM? The logging arch was abandoned on a farm in Lister, BC, about ten kilometres from Creston. In 1960, it was bought by the owners of a small private museum in Yahk, just east of Creston. When that museum went bankrupt, the Creston Museum bought its collection, including the logging arch.

WHO USED IT? Charles O. Rodgers, owner of the Canyon City Lumber Company, started his sawmill in 1908 and had at least two of these logging arches by 1913.

Kootenay/Rocky Mountains
› THE CRESTON MUSEUM AND ARCHIVES
LOGGING ARCH

Photo: The Creston Museum & Archives

Tell Me More

Logging used to be done in the winter using snow or ice trails. With the invention of the logging arch, loggers could move logs at any time of year. To use the logging arch, the loggers laid a heavy chain on the ground, then rolled and stacked the logs at a 90-degree angle to the chain, keeping the chain near the front of the stack. To help them do this, they used hooks and pulleys.

A team of horses backed the logging arch over the pile of logs so one wheel was on either side of the logs. The horses were then unhooked. The chain was fastened over the arch's **axle** then the arch's tow bar was moved so that it pointed straight up. The ends of the logging chain looped over two hooks on the axle.

When the tow bar was pulled down into its proper position, the front end of the logs lifted off the ground. The horses were hitched to the tow bar and started dragging the logs.

WOULD YOU BELIEVE?

This machine can move a pile of logs almost 1.5 metres high and 30 metres long. Thirty metres is about the distance between first and second base on a baseball field.

My Turn

Imagine you lived in a time before electricity or motors. Could you create a simple machine to move heavy objects?

CONNECTIONS

The early way of moving large stones
Photo: The Creston Museum & Archives

The logging arch was invented to move heavy logs during the late 19th and early 20th centuries. But logs are not the only heavy things that people needed to move. In the Neolithic or New Stone Age, many

European cultures buried their dead in graves dug into the ground and topped by a large heavy stone called a capstone. They had to move stones weighing

A Neolithic grave with a capstone

around 32 tonnes (about the weight of ten SUVs) without modern machinery. So how did they do this? One way they may have moved the stones was to lay logs end to end to form parallel tracks – a little like railway tracks. Then they would put several logs across these rails. The large stones were hoisted onto these logs and rolled along the rails.

⭐ WHY IS THE LOGGING ARCH IMPORTANT IN THIS AREA?

It wasn't until the 1850s that logging became a serious industry in British Columbia. When the Canadian Pacific Railway went through, logs could be shipped more easily to the east and to the United States. Any equipment that made getting logs to sawmills or places where they could be shipped to other locations easier played an important part in the area. By 1917, BC produced more wood than any other province. By the late 1920s, the province produced half of all the timber in Canada.

Logging operations in British Columbia in 1880
Source: New Westminster Museum, photographer unknown

JUST THE FACTS

WHAT IS IT? These military medals, paybooks and sergeant's stripes make up a display telling the story of the 230th Canadian Forestry Battalion.

WHAT DOES IT LOOK LIKE? Altogether, the collection takes up a space just about ten centimetres square. If you folded a piece of paper in four, that's about how big the collection is.

WHERE DOES IT COME FROM? Jack S. Watson, whose father Percy served in the 230th Forestry Battalion in the First World War, donated this collection of military objects to the Creston Museum.

WHO USED IT? Percy Watson lived and worked with his parents on a fruit ranch in Creston. He was also a skilled carpenter. Percy enlisted with the 230th Forestry Battalion in January 1917. He was appointed sergeant before the battalion left Creston and kept that rank overseas.

Tell Me More

When you think about war, you probably think about fighting, not logging. But during the First World War, the British and Canadian armies needed many things made out of wood like crates, supports for trench walls and rail ties. Wood was the most important building material. At the beginning of the war, wood was sent from Canada to Britain and France on ships. But the wood took up a lot of space that could have been used for food, medical supplies, weapons and, of course, soldiers.

› THE CRESTON MUSEUM AND ARCHIVES

230TH FORESTRY BATTALION: SERVICE MEDALS, PAYBOOKS AND SERGEANT'S STRIPES

In 1916, the British and Canadian High Command decided to recruit loggers and sawmill operators from Canada. These men formed special military units called Forestry Battalions. They cut down trees in England, Scotland and France. The trees were then squared and sawed, ready for use. By the end of the war, over 17,000 Canadian men were serving in the Forestry Corps.

Percy Watson's service with the 41st Company took him to Brittany in northwestern France and gave him lots of opportunities to talk with French people. His French became so good that later in life he could pass for a Frenchman with a Brittany accent – which he frequently did.

CONNECTIONS

During the Second World War, New Zealand sent three forestry companies to supply wood for the war effort. A "company" has between 80 and 150 soldiers. These soldiers took over sawmills that already existed and also built new mills.

The New Zealanders cut down several different types of trees, many of them very old. Imagine this. Some of the oak and chestnut trees they harvested were planted in 1805. That means they were around 135 years old when they were cut down by the foresters.

A New Zealander Forestry Corps
Photo: The Creston Museum & Archives

What do you think are the advantages and disadvantages of being part of a Forestry Battalion during a war?

⭐ WHY IS THE FORESTRY BATTALION IMPORTANT IN THIS AREA?

The 230th Forestry Battalion was created in Creston. Its commanding officer, Major Edward Mallandaine, had lived in Creston for 20 years, and many of the men who signed up were local.

Watson and Crookston embarking

Photo: The Creston Museum & Archives

Some men who joined the 230th Forestry Battalion had been rejected when they tried to enlist for the **infantry**. They might have been too old, or too young, or maybe not fit enough. Because the Forestry Battalion was not going to fight on the front lines, the requirements were a little less strict. Men were given a chance to serve their country using their skills with wood.

The Forestry Battalion was seen as a "safe" way of fighting the war. But these men still risked injury and death chopping down trees and working in sawmills. They lived in very poor conditions with little food. When the Allies needed more men for the final push that won the war, they called on some of the men from the Forestry Battalion to fight on the front lines. A few, including Everet Fortier, who also enlisted in Creston, were killed in battle.

16 TOUCHSTONES NELSON: MUSEUM OF ART AND HISTORY

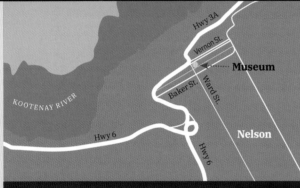

Museum

KOOTENAY RIVER

Nelson

Hwy 3A
Vernon St.
Baker St.
Ward St.
Hwy 6
Hwy 6

JUST THE FACTS

WHERE IS IT? 502 Vernon Street, Nelson, BC, V1L 4E7; (250) 352-9813
touchstonesnelson.ca

ARE PHOTOGRAPHS ALLOWED? Yes.

HOW DID IT START? The museum, also known as the Nelson and District Museum, Archives, Art Gallery and Historical Society, started in 1955 with the formation of the Kootenay Museum Association.

WHERE HAS IT LIVED?

The museum started in the old post office in the 1950s before moving ten years later to 618 Lake Street. This abandoned house had been the site of a successful business establishment run by a local woman, Rosie Ayres. In 1974, the museum moved into a newly built location, but the Nelson and District Museum, Archives, Art Gallery and Historical Society wanted a larger and more central location. Nearly 50 years after it first opened, the museum, archives and art gallery moved back into the newly renovated post office.

WHERE DO THE ITEMS COME FROM?

Most of the items come from the local community. Items must relate to Nelson's local history, and the museum has to make sure it can properly care for anything donated.

HOW HAS IT CHANGED?

One important change for the museum in Nelson was a name change in 2006 to "Touchstones." In the ancient world, a touchstone was used to test the quality of precious metals like gold and silver.

Touchstones measure excellence, and that's what the Nelson museum wants you to see. The name also reflects Nelson's mining history and the beautiful stone building it's housed in.

Museum staff are working with local First Nations communities to change educational programs and exhibits. They are following the United Nations Declaration on the Rights of Indigenous Peoples and answering the calls to action of the Truth and Reconciliation Commission of Canada.

NELSON DAILY NEWS COLLECTION

The *Nelson Daily News* was delivered as far west as the Okanagan, and as far east as southern Alberta.

The collection consists of over 50,000 newspapers published by the *Nelson Daily News* between 1902 and 2010.

It employed reporters, photographers, ad salespeople, editors, typesetters, press operators and paper carriers, just to name a few.

The composing room

For many years, the *Daily News* was Nelson's only newspaper and the main print source for news stories and opinions on local, national and international events.

The *Nelson Daily News* Business Office 1913

Nelson Daily News, Baker Street, 1950s

Before the internet, many people learned about what was happening in their community and around the world by reading newspapers once or twice a day.

The *Nelson Daily News* Business Office 1913

L-R: MacDonald, H.C. Grizzello, E.J. Patch, A.J. Dill

Although the news was fact-checked by an editor, stories could still be biased. Many stories reflected the opinions of the newspaper's owners and editors.

The collection assistant removing one of the hard bound books.

The newspapers are bound between hard covers, so the delicate paper is protected.

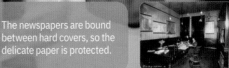

JUST THE FACTS

EDGAR DEWDNEY'S LIEUTENANT-GOVERNOR'S UNIFORM

WHAT IS IT? This suit was the uniform worn by British Columbia's Lieutenant-Governor from 1892 to 1897, 27 years after BC became Canada's sixth province.

WHAT DOES IT LOOK LIKE? This is a fancy uniform. Down the front and around the collar and cuffs of the jacket the tailor has applied heavy braiding made of gold and copper. The back of the jacket has long tails. The uniform also comes with a hat called a bicorn. The hat, like the coat, is decorated with gold and copper braid but also with feathers.

WHERE DOES IT COME FROM? The Dewdney family donated the uniform to the museum.

WHO USED IT? Edgar Dewdney wore this uniform while he was Lieutenant-Governor of BC.

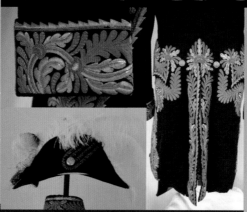

Tell Me More

Dewdney is a Canadian historical figure. He was an engineer and politician in the late 1800s. Dewdney's story is difficult, and it's important to know all parts of his story. Before he was the Lieutenant-Governor of British Columbia, Dewdney was the Indian commissioner and the Lieutenant-Governor of the North-West Territories (which at that time included both Alberta and Saskatchewan) from 1879 to 1888. At the same time, the Canadian Pacific Railway (CPR) was building the rail system from the eastern Canada to the west. Many First Nations and Métis people lived in the area of Cypress Hills, Saskatchewan. Because this land was sacred to them, they wished to make it their reserve. The government treaties stated that Indigenous people could choose their reserve lands, but the politicians and the CPR wanted the Indigenous people out of the area where the rail line was being built. On orders from Prime Minister John A. MacDonald, Dewdney refused to grant Indigenous people the land and closed Fort Walsh, which distributed food rations to the Indigenous people in this area. Buffalo, the main food source, had been overhunted, so many Indigenous people depended on these rations. By keeping food from the local First Nations, Dewdney hoped they would move north to where food rations were available. Thousands of First Nations people starved as a result of this action.

My Turn

Why do you think it's important for all of us to study the negative parts of Canadian history, as well as its positive parts?

WHY IS THE UNIFORM IMPORTANT IN THIS AREA?

Edgar Dewdney oversaw construction in the 1860s of what is now called "The Dewdney Trail," a 400-kilometre mule trail between Hope, BC, and Galbraith Ferry on the Kootenay River. Indigenous peoples had already created many routes to allow travel and trade from the ocean to the prairies. Dewdney used these established trails when planning his route.

CONNECTIONS

From workers in the fast food industry to firefighters, uniforms let us know who a person works for and what that person does. But uniforms do not mean the same thing to all people. For those who are sports fans, team uniforms represent heroes for some and opponents for others. While a police uniform should tell us we're safe, for many people, especially those who have been mistreated or oppressed by law enforcers, a police uniform is frightening.

Sinixt Traditional Territory.
Source: P. Pryce, Keeping the Lakes' Way

He also set off a chain of events that contributed to the Canadian government declaring the Sinixt First Nation extinct. In 1861, land at the mouth of the Kootenay River near Castlegar was set aside as a reserve by Gold Commissioner W. G. Cox. This land, called kp'itl'els, had been the traditional lands of the local First Nations for thousands of years. The reserve was never officially registered, and when Dewdney came through the area, he set this same land aside as a townsite. The property was bought and sold three times without the knowledge of the Christian

Alex Christian ("Indian Alex"), 1914.

family, the First Nations family who were living there and believed the land had been set aside as a reserve. The Christians were encouraged to move to the Oatscott Reserve on Arrow Lake but refused. The soil was poor, and they had no connection to it. They, like many other Sinixt people, were eventually forced to leave Canada and joined the Colville Band in Washington state.

JUST THE FACTS

WHAT IS IT? This nuclear fallout shelter was secretly constructed in the basement of a building called "The Gray Building" in 1964.

WHAT DOES IT LOOK LIKE? The entrance is through a steel bolt door – which lets you know it must have been pretty important. It has decontamination showers in case a person has come in contact with radioactive materials. The main room has a kitchen and a portable charcoal stove. Off this room are three dorm rooms, originally with bunk beds and two washrooms.

WHERE DOES IT COME FROM? The bunker was abandoned in the 1990s. In 2018, the museum leased the bunker from the owners of the Gray Building and now uses the space for exhibitions, collection storage and programs.

WHO USED IT? If there had been a nuclear attack, 70 local officials could have lived here for up to two weeks. This is how long some authorities believed it would take for the air to be safe. These "officials" would have included radio communication specialists, teletype operators, the heads of emergency services, members of government and military liaison officers. Unfortunately, it is clear that women did not hold important positions in those days. There was only a small dorm room for women and two large dorm rooms for men.

› TOUCHSTONES NELSON: MUSEUM OF ART AND HISTORY

1950s NUCLEAR BOMB SHELTER

Inside the bunker

Inspection tour of rations 1974

Dorm beds

For over 20 years, the Nelson bunker was restocked every two years with new emergency food packages. Why do you think this happened?

Feeding Unit Case 2

Tell Me More

The Nelson bunker, or as it was officially known, the "Kootenay Zonal Emergency Government Headquarters," was one of around 50 nuclear bomb shelters built across Canada during the **Cold War**. The prime minister of Canada at that time was John Diefenbaker. He had the bunkers built to make sure that governments across Canada could still function if there was a nuclear war. The main federal government fallout shelter near Ottawa was nicknamed the "Diefenbunker."

The shelter is not pretty. It's definitely not a place you'd like to spend months or years. It was designed to be **functional** and to provide safety. As well as the dorm rooms and washrooms, there's a supply room, an electrical room and a communications room with an office. Popular colours in the 1960s were yellow and orange, and the walls, doors and features are painted these colours.

The bunker still has the original water tanks, while the generator (to make electricity) and air circulation unit were recently renovated to meet current-day standards for public use.

My Turn

Living in a bunker during or after a nuclear war would have been like living in lockdown during the COVID-19 pandemic in 2020. What activities would you do while living in a bunker to keep yourself occupied and not bored, especially if your electronic devices wouldn't work and there was no TV or internet?

CONNECTIONS

While Nelson's bunker could house 70 people and was not very large, some of the secret bunkers in Canada were huge. Canadian Forces Station Carp, which was outside Ottawa, was 100,000 square feet (nearly 10,000 square metres), or almost twice the size of a football field. It was designed to allow 535 people to survive for 30 days. There were between 100 and 150 people employed in this bunker between 1962 and 1994. These people made sure the bunker was ready at all times in case of a nuclear war.

WHY IS THE BUNKER IMPORTANT IN THIS AREA?

Nelson was just one of the small towns chosen for a government shelter. Small towns were chosen for bunkers because the government thought the enemy would target big cities before small towns. Secrecy was important during construction of these bunkers, so secret that the project had a code name: Project EASE (Experimental Army Signals Establishment). It's hard to know how many people in Nelson knew about the bunker in the '60s, but as of 2013, when it was opened to the public for the first time, the secret was out.

17 CASTLEGAR STATION MUSEUM

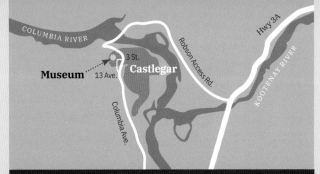

COLUMBIA RIVER

Hwy 3A

Robson Access Rd.

KOOTENAY RIVER

3 St.

Castlegar

Museum ···· 13 Ave.

Columbia Ave.

JUST THE FACTS

WHERE IS IT? 400 13th Avenue, Castlegar, BC, V1N 1G2; (250) 365-6440
stationmuseum.ca

ARE PHOTOGRAPHS ALLOWED? Yes.

HOW DID IT START? After a fire burned Castlegar's original train station to the ground in 1907, a new station was built. That's the building used for the museum today. The train station closed to the public in 1987, and the building was going to be torn down. The Castlegar Heritage Society, which had already preserved another historic site in the area – Zuckerberg Island – was determined to save the building and turn it into a museum. The City of Castlegar also played an important part in preserving Castlegar's history.

WHERE HAS IT LIVED?

While there were other museums in Castlegar, the Castlegar Heritage Society has had museums only in the station and at Zuckerberg Island Heritage Park, which has a small chapel house that houses the history of Alexander Zuckerberg and the Indigenous people.

The station building had to be lifted over the tracks from property that belonged to the Canadian Pacific Railway to property that belonged to the City of Castlegar, where the museum now lives.

The building was restored so it looks like it did in the 1930s. There's a baggage room, ticket room, waiting room and station master's living space.

As well as the station, the museum includes a caboose and a police station and jail. The British Columbia Provincial Police station and jail were used until the 1950s. The building was moved from its original location to the museum property.

WHERE DO THE ITEMS COME FROM?

Everything has been donated from local collections. While some items are very common – they could be found almost anywhere in British Columbia – all of them could have been used in the Castlegar area.

HOW HAS IT CHANGED?

Both the jail and the caboose are newer additions to the museum.

In a museum you can:

learn how some old technologies become popular again

PORTABLE ELECTROHOME RECORD PLAYER

This record player, which is about the size of a small desktop printer and weighs about six kilograms, was built in the 1950s.

It was the first portable record player you could carry to a friend's house to play your own music (not the stuff your parents listened to).

In the 1970s, people started buying their music on tapes then, later, on CDs so records went out of fashion for many years.

Many companies are now making turntables that look similar to the one you see in this museum.

Records that turned at 45 revolutions per minute were popular with teenagers in the '50s.

To play a "45" on the portable record player you see here, you had to put a little plastic piece into the hole.

The plastic piece was called a "spider" and was usually yellow or red.

Today, records have once again become popular, although not 45s.

JUST THE FACTS

DIVING SUIT

WHAT IS IT? This is a suit that allowed a diver to work and breathe underwater.

WHAT DOES IT LOOK LIKE? The suit is made from a kind of canvas. But the things you will notice most are the metal helmet with the four little windows and the giant metal shoes. This diving suit is the size of a very tall person. It weighs about 86 kilograms.

WHERE DOES IT COME FROM? This diving suit was used by Frank Frisby, and was donated by the West Kootenay Power Company.

WHO USED IT? It might seem strange to see what looks like a deep-sea diving suit in a place over 600 kilometres from the nearest ocean, but anyone working underwater in the early 20th century would have used this type of suit.

Tell Me More

With big metal shoes and a huge metal helmet, a diver wearing this diving suit looked a little like a monster or a strange astronaut. The weight of the shoes and the helmet made it possible for the diver to walk along the bottom of the river, lake or ocean.

Sharp rocks, metal edges and jagged pieces of wood could all puncture the suit, and a diver needed the suit to be waterproof. To help prevent rips and

punctures, manufacturers made the diving suit tough by lining the heavy canvas with rubber. The helmet was made of copper. This one has four vision ports – little windows the diver could use to look out of the helmet – and 12 bolts that attach the helmet to the suit.

So how did the diver breathe? It took two men to operate a pump that pumped fresh air into Frank's helmet while he worked underwater.

WOULD YOU BELIEVE?

It took six men to make sure Frank could do his job safely. Besides the two who kept the diver breathing, two men were needed to help Frank into and out of the water. He worked from a floating platform or raft. To get into the water, he would put on all of his equipment except his helmet and, with assistance, climb down a ladder. Just before he went under the water, one of the helpers would bolt his helmet to his suit, making sure there were no leaks. He would then be lowered into the water. When he came out, he had to be raised up again. The most important person was the one who talked on a telephone to Frank from the raft.

My Turn

Japanese *ama* divers are women who "free dive." This means they dive underwater to about nine metres deep without oxygen tanks. They hold their breath until they are about to come to the surface. As they are coming to the surface, they let out a long, slow whistle. If you were to write an advertisement for the *ama*, what slogan would you make up to attract tourists to where they dive?

Ama diver.
Photo: Wikimsedia Common, Fg2

CONNECTIONS

Over 200 years before Frank Frisby wore the diving suit you see here in the museum, a French man who served in the French navy invented a suit that could be used underwater. In 1715, Pierre Rémy de Beauve created a suit made of leather topped by a metal helmet with two hoses coming out of the top. Fresh air was pumped into one hose, and used air went out the other.

Pierre Remy de Beauve's diving suit

Pierre de Rémy de Beauve. Projet pour l'équipement d'un plongeur. Ensemble de six dessins, 1715. Dessin, encre, aquarelle sur papier (43,5 x 54 cm). Paris, Archives nationales, Cartes, Plans et Photographies, Marine, 6 JJ 89 (p. 119B et C)

⭐ WHY IS THE DIVING SUIT IMPORTANT IN THIS AREA?

West Kootenay Power and Light built three dams in the early 1900s: the Lower Bonnington, Corra Linn and Brilliant dams. Divers were used for any underwater work needed during dam construction. Divers were also used for underwater inspections and maintenance work.

Modern diving suits are much more sophisticated than their earlier cousins.
Photo: Wikimedia Commons: Marco Busdraghi

JUST THE FACTS

WHAT IS IT? This building housed Castlegar's first police detachment.

WHAT DOES IT LOOK LIKE? Not only is there a place for police officers to work in this building, there is also a jail where people would be held for a short time before they were released or sent to a prison. The office space was also used as a court.

WHERE DOES IT COME FROM? When the museum obtained the building, it was no longer a police station. It was a garage. The land it was sitting on was expropriated – that means it was taken by the government for a project it had planned. In this case, the government was building a new bridge. The landowner informed the museum that the building was available.

WHO USED IT? The British Columbia Provincial Police used the building from 1934 until 1950. Then the BCPP was absorbed into the Royal Canadian Mounted Police. The RCMP used the building for another nine years.

Tell Me More

When the BCPP was first created in 1858, just before Confederation, there was one officer to patrol over 900,000 square kilometres. Remember there were no motorized vehicles back then, only horses and mules. How do you think he would have done his job? Eventually, the BCPP grew to over 500 officers.

CASTLEGAR POLICE STATION AND JAIL

CONNECTIONS

Norfolk Island on the globe

Image: Wikimedia Commons, TUBS

Even very small places have police stations and jails. For example, Norfolk Island, which lies 1400 kilometres off the coast of Australia, is only 34.6 square kilometres in size. That's one-third the size of the City of Vancouver. But Norfolk Island has a police station and jail. Not all jails will look the same around the world, but nearly all societies have someplace to keep people who have disobeyed the law.

The first Castlegar BCPP detachment (that means a smaller unit within the larger police force) started in the building you see on the museum property today. When the museum relocated the building, it was renovated to look the way it did in the 1950s. The original jail cells remain in the building, as well as many objects donated by the family of the first police constable in Castlegar, Constable George MacAndrew.

★ WHY IS THE POLICE STATION AND JAIL IMPORTANT IN THIS AREA?

This police station and the men who worked here played an important part in the history of this town. Being able to see the police station as it was gives us an idea of what it was like to live in this small town in the mid-20th century. The station housed the police detachment, the jail and the courthouse, all in one building.

As you can see, this police station had many functions. Once a couple even got married here. In 1957, a police constable, Corporal Macdonald, who, as a justice of the peace, was allowed to conduct weddings, was scheduled to marry Bud and Iris Beauchamp. The wedding was supposed to be held at Macdonald's house, but his house became unavailable. He married the young couple at the police station instead.

18 NIKKEI INTERNMENT MEMORIAL CENTRE

JUST THE FACTS

WHERE IS IT? 306 Josephine Street, New Denver, BC, V0G 1S1
(250) 358-7288
newdenver.ca/nikkei/

ARE PHOTOGRAPHS ALLOWED? Yes.

HOW DID IT START? The New Denver Kyowakai Society created the Nikkei Internment Memorial Centre between 1992 and 1994. The Japanese internment camps were places where the Canadian government forced Japanese Canadian people to move from the west coast of Canada during the Second World War. The government said it was worried about threats to the security of Canada after Pearl Harbor was bombed by Japan. Many of the Japanese people interned were born in Canada. The government took their property and did not return it after the war. In 1988, the Canadian government formally apologized to Japanese Canadian survivors and their families.

This site is one of the very few that was not torn down after the war. The memorial preserves buildings and objects from the internment camp to remind us that, between 1942 and 1957, the Canadian government stripped Japanese Canadian people of their civil rights, labelled them "enemy aliens" and forced them to evacuate the west coast and live in detention camps. The centre helps us all learn about the internees' experiences.

SLOCAN LAKE

Hwy 31A

Hwy 6

New Denver

2 Ave.

Museum

Hwy 6

WHERE HAS IT LIVED?

Where the memorial sits was once a large piece of land used to grow vegetables and fruit. The area was called "The Orchard." The camp was built on the site by the Canadian government under the authority of the British Columbia Security Commission to house forced evacuees. The memorial opened on the original site of the detention camp.

WHERE DO THE ITEMS COME FROM?

Some of the buildings and items are from this site. The outhouse is the only building that has been reconstructed. The Kyowakai Hall is in its original location, but the office, the 1942 shack and 1957 shack have been moved to their current locations from elsewhere in the Orchard.

All of the buildings and the items in the collection have been donated.

HOW HAS IT CHANGED?

New items continue to be donated to the collection. The Heiwa Teien garden designed by Roy (Tomomichi) Sumi was not in the original camp. In 2007, the memorial centre was named a National Historic Site of Canada.

In a museum you can:

learn how many interned Japanese used their traditional footwear to adapt to hardship conditions

GETA

Over 22,000 Japanese Canadian men, women and children were interned during and even after the Second World War.

Geta is a style of Japanese footwear often worn with a kimono. These geta belonged to a man.

The shoes are raised slightly off the ground with a thick wooden sole.

Some geta worn by women have one or two wooden blocks attached to the soles of the shoes.

In Japanese, these blocks are called ha, which means "teeth." When you look at geta from the side, the wooden blocks look like teeth.

Walkways were often muddy and the areas around the bath and wash houses very wet. The geta were useful shoes to wear in these conditions.

Many of these internment camps were in British Columbia in places where the winters are cold and the summers hot.

Images: Nikkei Internment Memorial Centre

JUST THE FACTS

WHAT IS IT? The *ofuro* is a Japanese bathtub. Many of the cabins in the internment camps did not have private baths so tubs were built that could be shared by several families.

WHAT DOES IT LOOK LIKE? The shapes might differ slightly, but generally the ofuro was square or rectangular with steep sides. It was made from cedar planks with cotton batting pushed between the planks to make it waterproof. On one side of the tub, an old hot water tank or a metal barrel was used as a stove to heat the water. Cedar slats between where bathers sat and the tank kept bathers from burning themselves on the hot metal.

WHERE DOES IT COME FROM? The Kyowakai centre is the only building on the memorial's site that served as an ofuro (the traditional Japanese bath).

WHO USED IT? Everyone in the internment camp used an ofuro, but probably not as often as they wished they could.

› NIKKEI INTERNMENT MEMORIAL CENTRE

OFURO

Tell Me More

It may seem strange to you that more than one person would share bath water. Remember that conditions in these internment camps were very primitive. Heat and running water were not always available. You might be asking, "Wouldn't the water get dirty?" To make sure that didn't happen, each person using the ofuro would wash before getting into the tub. It is not uncommon in Japan for more than one person to use the same bath water, so it is forbidden to wash in the tub.

In the internment camps several families would have to share the ofuro. Some families would bathe together if the tub was large enough. You can understand why it was important for everyone to be clean before entering the tub.

Preparing the ofuro took time. Most of us turn on a tap and out comes hot water. This wasn't the case in most internment camps. Water for the ofuro had to be heated. If there wasn't running water, the water for the tub would have to be brought up from a lake or river.

There was little privacy in the internment camps. You couldn't lock a bathroom door and soak in the bathtub for 30 or 40 minutes. Many of the showering and bathing areas were common, which meant sharing with many people you would not necessarily know. How would you feel about that?

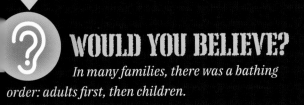

WOULD YOU BELIEVE?

In many families, there was a bathing order: adults first, then children.

Communal baths are not uncommon. In Iceland, because of the volcanic nature of the island, there are many hot springs. These hot springs are where people gather with their families or meet up with friends after work.

Like a bathtub, these pools do not have chemicals to keep them clean. There are strict rules about washing your whole body, including your hair, with soap and water before entering the pool. If everyone follows the rules, the water stays clean.

Iceland is famous for its natural hot springs and public bathing.

My Turn

Many Japanese Canadian families were separated during the war. Mothers and older female children were left in charge of the cooking, childcare, cleaning and laundry, as well as looking after the family's finances. Knowing about the poor conditions in the camp, how would all of these activities have been harder?

WHY IS THE OFURO IMPORTANT IN THIS AREA?

The Nikkei Internment Memorial Centre in New Denver is only a small part of the original centre that housed over 1,500 people. Not all these people used this one ofuro, but seeing the tub reminds us that a number of people did share the bathing area. It is important to remember that the Japanese Canadian people who were interned were used to the same modern conveniences and comforts as everyone else. How hard it must have been to survive in these camps without the privacy that most of us are used to and with the most basic tools and materials to build the bare necessities of life.

Photo: Nikkei Internment Memorial Centre

JUST THE FACTS

WHAT IS IT? A *mochi mallet* looks like a hammer made out of wood. It is used to pound a special kind of rice into rice balls or mochi.

WHAT DOES IT LOOK LIKE? The handle looks a little like a fat broom handle. The head of the mallet is cylindrical. It is made from two pieces of wood and fastened with nails. The mochi mallets that were made in internment camps were not all the same. Their sizes depended on what wood and what tools were available to the woodworker.

WHERE DOES IT COME FROM? The mochi mallet, also called a pestle, was found in a house called the Ono house.

WHO USED IT? The mallet was used to pound rice. Anyone could have used this mallet, but beating rice in a mortar is very hard work. Consequently, it was often done by adults.

Pounding Mochi into paste

Mochi is eaten in many different forms, including as candy and ice-cream.
Wikimedia Commons, Aurus Sy

› NIKKEI INTERNMENT MEMORIAL CENTRE

MOCHI MALLET

WOULD YOU BELIEVE?

Have you ever seen the shapes of animals or peoples' faces in the clouds? When you look at the moon, can you see the man in the moon? According to Japanese folklore, the shape on the moon is a moon rabbit or moon hare. The rabbit is pounding mochi with a mallet.

My Turn

Use the internet to look up the fastest mochi maker in the world. If you were to write a job description for a mochi maker, what would you say?

Pounded yam is a traditional food in Nigeria. Yams and rice have something in common. Both are very glutinous – that means they are very sticky. The yams are peeled and boiled and then put into a mortar, just like the mochigome rice. They are crushed with a wooden pestle that looks more like a baseball bat than a hammer. When all the lumps are gone, and the yams are smooth and stretchy, water is added. Like mochi, the beaten yams are shaped into balls. Pounded yams are most often eaten by pinching a piece from the ball and dipping it into a soup.

WHY IS THE MOCHI MALLET IMPORTANT IN THIS AREA?

Mochitsuki is the annual tradition of pounding rice to make mochi. It takes place around New Year. Today, many Japanese people will buy mochi from the store, but during the Second World War, when Japanese Canadians were interned here in New Denver and elsewhere, mochitsuki would have been an important way to celebrate together as a family and a community.

Mochitsuki is an old tradition
Image: Wikimedia Commons, A.Davey

Tell Me More

Can you name any food that has to be beaten before it is served? Mochi is one of those foods. To make mochi, a special kind of rice called *mochigome* must be used. It is very sticky. It is soaked overnight, then steamed, then put into a mortar. The rice is pounded using the mallet until it is a soft, smooth, stretchy ball. Mochi can be sweet or **savoury** depending on the ingredients that are added.

It takes at least two people to make mochi: the pounder who uses the mallet, and someone who flips the rice and adds water so the rice doesn't stick to the mallet or the mortar. This second job is quite dangerous. Being hit by a mallet can cause serious injury.

Japanese Canadians were not allowed to take much with them to the internment camps, so it's likely that mallets and mortars were left behind. They were heavy and bulky. While the Japanese Canadians were held in the detention camps, someone would have handmade both the mallets and the mortar. But getting the correct type of rice would have been a challenge. We know that at one point the Japanese Red Cross sent some mochigome rice to Canada. Frank Maikawa, who was a child interned with his parents near Lillooet, remembers his father and another man cutting down a tree and hollowing out a piece of the trunk to make a mortar. They also made the mallets to beat the rice.

19 ROSSLAND MUSEUM & DISCOVERY CENTRE

Photo: Rossland Museum & Discovery

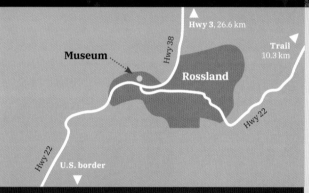

WHERE HAS IT LIVED?

When the federal government offered funds for projects that would celebrate Canada's 100th birthday, the Rossland Museum – backed by the community – put in a proposal for a new museum to be built on the site of the old Black Bear Mine. The group, including Rossland Rotary Club members, raised one-third of the funds with a number of fundraisers, including selling mining stock certificates at $1.00 each. The new museum opened in 1967, during Canada's centennial year. From 1967 to 2009, the museum also offered a tour through the Black Bear Mine entry tunnel.

WHERE DO THE ITEMS COME FROM?

The Rossland Museum accepts donated artifacts that were used in Rossland or by Rosslanders. Many of the large mining artifacts on the site have come from other local mine sites and were donated by the Consolidated Mining and Smelting Company, now Teck Trail Operations.

HOW HAS IT CHANGED?

Since 1967, there have been many changes. A theatre, new exhibition wings and new buildings and displays in the upper bench have been added. Permanent exhibits are regularly updated, and in 2017 a new entrance gallery and archives were built. A replica mine tunnel experience is planned to open in 2022.

The museum offers indoor, outdoor and downtown tours, as well as a variety of exciting children's programs and community events.

JUST THE FACTS

WHERE IS IT? 1100 BC-3B (Junction of Highways 3B and 22), Rossland, BC, V0G 1Y0; (250) 362-7722, or 888-448-7444
rosslandmuseum.ca

ARE PHOTOGRAPHS ALLOWED? Yes.

HOW DID IT START? The Rossland Rotary Club started the first museum in Rossland in 1954. It was housed in the basement of the Rossland Courthouse. This was the beginning of the Rossland Historical Museum and Archives Association, now the Rossland Museum & Discovery Centre.

In a museum you can:

learn about the history of chairlifts in British Columbia

RED MOUNTAIN CHAIRLIFT

Skiing was made popular in Rossland by Scandinavian miners in the 1890s and continued to grow over the years.

The chairlift at Red Mountain was the first in western Canada.

Engineers and avid skiers from the nearby Consolidated Mining and Smelting Company of Canada volunteered their expert knowledge of tramways to build the Red Mountain chairlift.

A large bull wheel attached to a tower at the top of the hill, and a tail pulley attached to a second tower at the bottom.

70 Single rider chairs on 2500 metres of cable moved up and down the mountain over 14 more towers.

The ride up took 11 minutes, and, if you changed your mind, you could just ride the chair back down.

Before the chairlift was built, skiers used a small rope tow to pull them up the mountain. Before that, they had to hike up every run!

Photo: Rossland Museum & Discovery Centre

JUST THE FACTS

WHAT IS IT? The Father Pat Memorial Ambulance is a horse-drawn ambulance.

WHAT DOES IT LOOK LIKE? The ambulance is about 1.5 metres wide and about 4.25 metres long. Today, you could just squeeze two of these ambulances side by side in a large single-car garage. A modern ambulance is almost twice as wide and twice as long.

WHERE DOES IT COME FROM? The ambulance was purchased in September 1902 with money from the Father Pat Memorial Fund. The community led a fundraising project to honour Father Pat , a beloved priest and community leader. It was donated to the Rossland Museum in 1974.

WHO USED IT? The ambulance served the community of Rossland and the surrounding area and operated out of the Rossland Fire Hall.

Kootenay/Rocky Mountains

› **ROSSLAND MUSEUM & DISCOVERY CENTRE**

FATHER PAT MEMORIAL AMBULANCE

Photo: Don Conway and Tourism Rosslan

CONNECTIONS

Not all ambulances travel on roads. In Australia, the Royal Flying Doctor Service flies doctors into remote areas of the country and brings patients who need special treatment to hospitals.

A man similar to Father Pat was responsible for creating the flying doctors. Reverend John Flynn was a Presbyterian missionary whose job it was to look after people in Australia's Outback. The Outback is a remote area in the interior part of Australia. Flynn set up hospitals in rural areas, but that didn't help people who lived far from those communities.

Lieutenant (John) Clifford Peel wrote Rev. Flynn a letter, saying he had seen a missionary doctor visit patients using a plane. Flynn took this idea and, in 1928, an injured miner was flown from a small mining town to a larger centre with medical services. This was the start of the flying doctors.

Don't you think Father Pat would have loved seeing something like that in Rossland?

My Turn

It's 1903 and you're the ambulance driver for the Father Pat Memorial Ambulance. What are some of the hazards of driving a horse-drawn ambulance on the hilly dirt roads of Rossland?

⭐ WHY IS THE AMBULANCE IMPORTANT IN THIS AREA?

Father Pat was a minister at St. George's Anglican Church. Although he was in Rossland for only three years (1896 – 1899), Rosslanders respected him for his constant caring and devotion to the community.

Father Pat passed away in Montreal in 1902, and when Rosslanders heard about his passing, they wanted to do something to honour his memory. This ambulance was purchased for the community in his memory after a fundraising campaign throughout 1902 that included contributions from many surrounding communities with memories of Father Pat.

Tell Me More

The ambulance was horse-drawn. Like today, people were transported or treated in the back of the ambulance. Can you imagine how bumpy a ride in this ambulance must have been? Roads were not paved, the horses did not provide a smooth ride like a car engine and the springs could not make up for the many potholes and ruts in the road.

JUST THE FACTS

WHAT IS IT? A bull wheel is part of a pulley system that can raise and lower large heavy loads.

WHAT DOES IT LOOK LIKE? The bull wheel is about four metres in diameter. That's almost twice as long as a king-sized bed. Its edge has teeth. There is a long metal axle that runs through a hole in the middle of the wheel. Some of the teeth along the edge of the bull wheel are missing.

WHERE DOES IT COME FROM? This bull wheel comes from the War Eagle Mine, one of the five major mines on Red Mountain.

WHO USED IT? The operator who ran the hoist attached to the bull wheel would definitely have been a man, since women were not allowed to work underground until 1978. This bull wheel was last used in 1899.

› ROSSLAND MUSEUM & DISCOVERY CENTRE

WAR EAGLE MINE BULL WHEEL

Photo: Rossland Museum & Discovery Centre

Tell Me More

This bull wheel was one part of the War Eagle Mine's electric (**pneumatic**) hoist system.

A hoist raised and lowered a cage, or **skip**, through a mine shaft. Bull wheels like this one would wind or unwind the cable attached to the cage or skip. A cage usually carried men and equipment, while a skip moved ore out of a mine.

WOULD YOU BELIEVE?

You will notice that the teeth on this bull wheel have been destroyed. The man who managed the mine at the time of the accident reportedly broke the teeth to make sure no one could use the gear again.

My Turn

If you have a bicycle with more than one gear, can you figure out why you can coast on your bike without the pedals moving? Ask an adult to help you figure this out.

CONNECTIONS

Another name for a bull wheel is a "gear wheel." If you own a bicycle, you have something that looks like a gear wheel only much smaller. Do you remember your first bicycle? It probably had a toothed gear wheel in the front where your pedals were, and a smaller gear wheel, or cog, attached to the back wheel. The chain would have run around the front gear wheel and around the smaller back gear wheel – like a hoist cable would wind around a bull wheel. Pedalling made the rear bicycle wheel move. The faster you pedalled, the faster you could go. Even when you stopped pedalling, the pedals still moved. That's because the cog at the back was attached to the rear wheel.

WHY IS THE BULL WHEEL IMPORTANT IN THIS AREA?

Bull wheels are essential to the operation of the underground mines to move people, supplies and rock. This bull wheel actually has a sad story. It was part of a major accident at the War Eagle Mine. A missing safety pin caused a bolt on the gear to slip out of place and the brake system failed. At the time, five men were using the skip to move to another part of the mine. They fell 107 metres to the bottom of the mine shaft. Four were killed and one was injured.

Even though none of the men had family in town, the entire community attended their funerals.

Cogs

THREE MEN KILLED!

A STRICT INQUIRY: in the War Eagle Morning.

The Coroner's War E

WAR EAGLE DISASTER

HULL STAT A Loose Nut Caused the Terrible Accident Yesterday

Time to Wonder

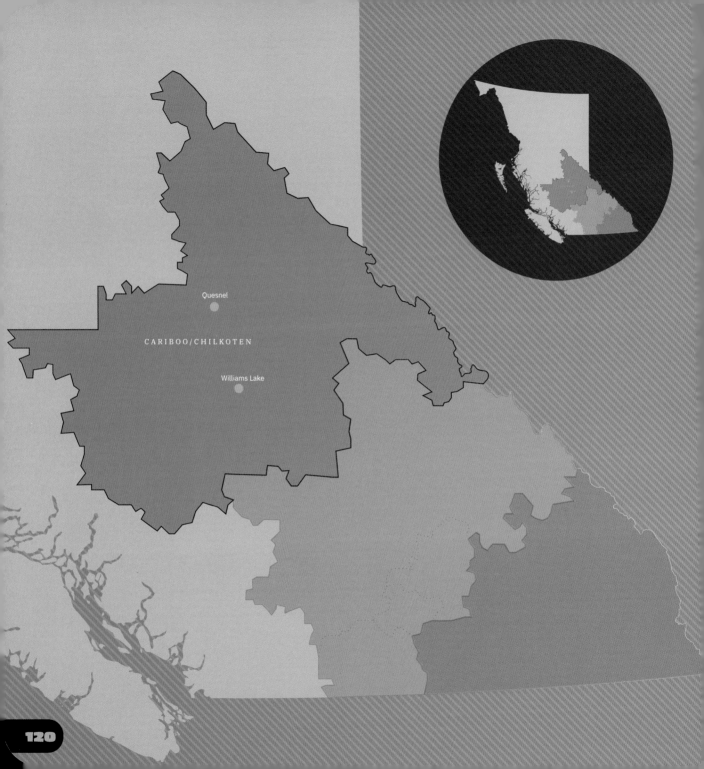

CARIBOO/CHILKOTEN

Quesnel

Williams Lake

CARIBOO CHILCOTIN

TRADITIONAL AND UNCEDED TERRITORY OF THE FOLLOWING FIRST NATIONS:

Dakelh

Lhtako Dené

Secwepemc

Tsilhqot'in

Cariboo Chilcotin

20 QUESNEL & DISTRICT MUSEUM AND ARCHIVES

JUST THE FACTS

WHERE IS IT? 705 Carson Avenue, Quesnel, BC, V2J 2B6; (250) 992-9580
quesnelmuseum.ca

ARE PHOTOGRAPHS ALLOWED? Yes.

HOW DID IT START? Before there was an actual building to call a museum in Quesnel, a group of locals interested in the town's history began putting together a collection of household items, farm machinery, mining and logging equipment and photographs. These belongings would eventually become the foundation of the museum's collection. In 1951, the same year as Disney's film *Alice in Wonderland* was released, the Cariboo Historical Society was formed. The society was allowed to use the basement of the Federal Building to store its artifacts. It took the society 12 years of fundraising and planning to build a small museum.

WHERE HAS IT LIVED?

In 1963, around the time, Disney's *The Sword in the Stone* was playing at the movies, the museum was opened in a joint facility with the new tourist information centre. In the beginning, society members and volunteers looked after the collection. Nine years later, the city officially took over. Over time, additions were added to create more space and innovative technologies adopted to make the story of Quesnel more approachable.

WHERE DO THE ITEMS COME FROM?

In the case of a community museum often by donation. People like the Boyd family, who, from the 1860s on, ran roadhouses along the Cariboo Wagon Road that prospectors, miners, settlers and travellers of all kinds stopped at. One of these was the Cottonwood House, which now is a museum, just east of Quesnel. When Harry Boyd sold it, he allowed historical society members to select many items.

The museum has a fine collection of items belonging to Quesnel's early Chinese settlers. Many contributed to this, but Bill Hong, Bob Barlow and the Hoy family are among the significant donors.

Long-time volunteer Veera Peever donated many items from her family, as well as pieces she collected specifically for the museum. At her 100th birthday party the museum staff prepared a special scavenger hunt. The challenge? To find just a few of the items she'd donated that were currently on display at the museum.

HOW HAS IT CHANGED?

Nowadays, museums want donations that tell a story about their community. Looking at a possible donation, the curator asks, "Who used it? Was it used here?"

In a museum you can:

see what a "selfie" used to look like

FAMILY PORTRAIT BY C. S. WING

Chinese Canadian photographer C. S. Wing (Chow Shong Wing) lived in Quesnel, British Columbia, from about 1907 to 1928.

The photograph is a new print from a glass plate negative.

Wing's photographs are an important record of the different types of people living in this small frontier town.

Wing was a partner in his family's general store, the Wah Lee Company, which was founded in the 1860s during the Cariboo Gold Rush.

Wing added the photography business as a sideline.

He took portraits of visitors and local residents from all walks of life. Perhaps because of his role as the local shopkeeper, or his own minority status, he was able to work with all cultures.

For many years this picture was nicknamed "The Fur Family photo" by the museum staff because the identity of the family was a mystery.

A museum researcher was able to match birth records and newspaper stories that suggested an identity. The man could be Thomas Fox, an Englishman, who in 1913 arrived in Quesnel with his wife, Mary, and their children to manage the local Hudson's Bay store.

Over time, Wing's untouched negatives have degraded, giving some of the portraits an eerie feel like something belonging in a ghost movie.

JUST THE FACTS

WHAT IS IT? The Royal Bank's bathtub is a classic cast iron tub. Tubs like these usually weigh between 90 and 180 kilograms. To put this in perspective, a blue whale's heart weighs about 181 kilograms. What would be the best way to move a weight like this? Four strong men, two large workhorses, an elephant, 500 fluffy bunnies?

WHAT DOES IT LOOK LIKE? Claw-foot tubs come in four classic shapes: roll rim tubs, also known as roll top tubs or flat rim tubs; slipper tubs named for the fact one end is raised and one sloped, perfect for lounging; double slipper tubs that feature ends that are both raised and sloped; and last but certainly not least, the double-ended tubs with two rounded ends. Take a look at the Royal Bank's bathtub and figure out what kind it is.

WHERE DOES IT COME FROM? The bathtub was used at the bank from 1928 to 1961. Even after it was no longer needed to keep staff clean, it made a pretty good ice bucket at parties.

One summer, when the bank manager was away, a customer offered to buy the bathtub for a house he was renovating, and his offer was accepted. In 1978, a landlord named Ed White was updating his rental property on Reid Street and offered the famous bathtub to the museum.

WHO USED IT? Everyone. In 1928, when the Royal Bank was built, only a few places in Quesnel had running water. The bank manager expected his employees to be very presentable, and since many of them lived in rented rooms, he decided the bank needed a full bathroom. It wasn't long until everyone in the area knew about the bank's fancy tub.

Cariboo Chilcotin
> QUESNEL & DISTRICT MUSEUM AND ARCHIVES

ROYAL BANK BATHTUB

WOULD YOU BELIEVE?

The bank's bath was so popular that, before any big social event, a schedule would have to be made up for all the bathers. Imagine having to wait for your entire street to have a bath before you got a turn. At least they used their own water.

CONNECTIONS

We owe a great deal of thanks to a man called John Michael Kohler for the bathtubs we enjoy today. Kohler owned a foundry in Wisconsin that made farming products like water troughs and hog scalders (generally, a large pot or tub used to remove the hair off a slaughtered pig) from cast iron and steel. In 1883, Kohler invented his first bathtub. He advertised it in a catalogue, saying, "A horse trough/hog scalder...when furnished with four legs will serve as a bathtub." It wasn't long before his business was completely devoted to tubs and other bathroom fixtures. Today, the name Kohler is known worldwide for its products.

My Turn

Like John Michael Kohler, a lot of inventors started by making one thing, only to invent another by accident. During the Second World War, chemist James Wright was trying to create a synthetic rubber substitute when he ended up inventing Silly Putty instead. Today, it's known as one of the best-selling toys ever.

Find out about other accidental inventors. Start with this article: "15 Life-Changing Inventions That Were Created by Mistake," from *Business Insider* (https://www.businessinsider.com/these-10-inventions-were-made-by-mistake-2010-11.) You'll be surprised by what you discover.

⭐ WHY IS THE TUB IMPORTANT IN THIS AREA?

The story is completely unique to Quesnel. It's a great local legend.

Tell Me More

Soon customers began to ask to use the tub. Quesnel was famous for being dusty, and many of its occupants worked tough physical jobs like ranching and mining. The chance to do their weekly banking and get a good wash was very popular.

These tubs were fashionable in the Victorian era and were considered the pinnacle of sophistication – in other words, very cool. Before the cast-iron tub, early Victorian bathtubs were made of zinc, tin or copper, with a wooden casing. Eventually, when indoor plumbing became common, the tub became less popular.

JUST THE FACTS

WHAT IS IT? This turban belonged to RCMP Officer Baltej Singh Dhillon. In 1990, he was the first RCMP officer to be allowed to wear a turban. His first posting was in Quesnel.

WHAT DOES IT LOOK LIKE? Just like the official RCMP hat, the official turban is navy blue with the official RCMP crest on it.

WHERE DOES IT COME FROM? Dhillon arranged for the turban to be donated to the museum in 1995, when he was transferring from the community after four years of service. Still, as it was his official uniform issued by the RCMP, the donor is listed as the Quesnel Detachment of the RCMP.

WHO USED IT? When Dhillon asked to wear his turban with his uniform, it created a huge debate. The public was split. Though Dhillon had many supporters, his opponents were determined. A businessman from Calgary had pins made to express his disapproval of the idea. Finally, after some months, Dhillon won his battle. Solicitor General Pierre Cadieux approved changes to the regulations governing the RCMP uniform.

Cariboo Chilcotin

> QUESNEL & DISTRICT MUSEUM AND ARCHIVES

INAUGURAL RCMP TURBAN

Baltej Dhillon: The man unde

© Baltej Singh Dhillon

CONNECTIONS

A *kippah*, also known as a yarmulke, is a circular cap worn by Jewish men on the back of their heads. Orthodox Jewish men wear one all the time as an act of dedication to god. Jewish men who are from Liberal or Reform denominations – subgroups inside Judaism – see it as noncompulsory. There are occasions when generally all Jewish men cover their heads, like during prayer, visiting a synagogue and religious events.

When non-Jewish men visit a synagogue, they're not required to cover their heads, though it's considered courteous. Often *kippah* are provided at big events like bar or bat mitzvahs and funerals, and at Jewish cemeteries.

⭐ WHY IS THE TURBAN IMPORTANT IN THIS AREA?

Dhillon's turban is a reminder of how even one person can make a difference. To the greater Indo-Canadian community, this turban is a symbol of strength, belief and courage.

For the first seven years of his career, Dhillon was the only Mountie who wore a turban. Finally, in the late '90s, another Sikh officer was posted to Burnaby. Dhillon was so happy when he found out that he called the man right away to express his excitement.

My Turn

Take a moment to think about how you describe yourself. Do you remember when you first noticed that not everyone looked the same? Can you recall a time when your identity made you proud or sad? Do you find these questions difficult to think about? If you were a teacher, how would you begin a conversation about racism with your class?

Tell Me More

Even after Cadieux had approved the changes, many people continued to argue against the new dress code. There were even anonymous death threats made against Dhillon.

By the time Dhillon retired from the RCMP in 2019, he'd risen to the rank of inspector. He was a specialist in interrogation and polygraph testing, and was involved in many high-profile cases, including the Air India bombing. Nowadays, he is still involved in law enforcement, working with the Combined Forces Special Enforcement Unit of British Columbia, an anti-gang agency.

Sikh turbans are made out of long strips of cotton or silk. The way they are wound is very precise. Turbans can be any colour. There are no rules. It's a choice. The style of one's turban is personal. The turban is a central part of the Sikh religion; it's not just symbolic. It's a practice that shows faith in god. For Sikhs, wearing a turban is obligatory. Being told not to wear a turban is the same as telling a Sikh to disrespect god. This is unthinkable to them. Sikhs always wear their turbans.

MUSEUM OF THE CARIBOO-CHILCOTIN

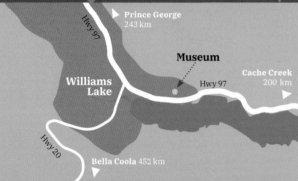

Prince George
243 km

Hwy 97

Museum

Williams Lake

Hwy 97

Cache Creek
200 km

Hwy 20

Bella Coola 452 km

JUST THE FACTS

WHERE IS IT? 1660 Broadway Avenue South, Williams Lake, BC, V2G 2W4; (250) 392-7404
cowboy-museum.com

ARE PHOTOGRAPHS ALLOWED? Yes.

HOW DID IT START? In 1967, the 100th anniversary of Canadian Confederation, the first Williams Lake Centennial Museum opened. Of course, it didn't just happen overnight. The idea for a museum had been brewing for many years, as far back as the early '50s. A local historical society started when it was discovered there was nowhere for a local donor to leave his belongings. Like today, the original museum shared its space with the tourist information centre.

WHERE HAS IT LIVED?

By the time hockey superstar Wayne Gretzky was named the top scorer in the history of the NHL, the space shared with the tourist information centre had become much too small for the museum. A new home was needed. Its next home was an old Health Unit building. Over the next two years, money was raised to renovate and update the building.

WHERE DO THE ITEMS COME FROM?

Most of the items here are donations.

HOW HAS IT CHANGED?

In 2017, the museum moved again to a large modern space that overlooks the lake. Once again, it shares space with the tourist information centre and the chamber of commerce in the beautiful log building called the Tourism Discovery Centre. These days, the museum occupies the basement level, which has been renovated and updated to help bring the stories of the Cariboo Chilcotin to life.

Photo: Museum of the Cariboo-Chilcotin

In a museum you can:

see why your grandma was afraid of the dentist

DR. BOTHAMLEY'S DENTIST CHAIR AND TOOL STAND

Dr. Bothamley's tool stand looks like a giant metal octopus, or a torture device used by a villain in an old sci-fi movie.

A Williams Lake family gave the chair to the museum in the 1990s. It was a fixture in the dentist's office during the '50s and '60s.

A local woman discovered the dentist tool stand, light and the accompanying pieces in the basement of an old building she managed. She immediately recognized them as Dr. Bothamley's. Her husband donated these pieces in the early 2000s.

At one time Dr. Bothamley was the only dentist in town. He looked after everyone in the community.

Before dentists like Dr. Bothamley began practising dentistry in Williams Lake in the early 1900s, residents had to travel to get their teeth looked after.

Mary Telfer, the museum's vice-president, was treated by Dr. Bothamley.

Dr. Bothamley's dental set features a foot pedal drill. A dentist uses a drill when preparing a tooth for a filling.

Today's drills are much faster than the drills used in the past. This is great news, as it means a visit to the dentist is a lot less painful and much faster.

JUST THE FACTS

WHAT IS IT? This saddle, owned by Lloyd "Cyclone" Smith, is a very fancy Western saddle that weighs about nine kilograms – about the same weight as a Jack Russell dog, or a car tire, or two big bags of potatoes.

WHAT DOES IT LOOK LIKE? It looks heavy. It's dark brown. It has all the regular Western saddle features, such as a horn, stirrups and a cantle (which is a fancy way of saying a high back to the seat).

WHERE DOES IT COME FROM? This special saddle passed through quite a few hands before reaching the museum. After Cyclone Smith's death, his Uncle Bill was left the saddle. He then sold it to a man called Harry Smith. He was no relation to Cyclone. Harry lived at 158 Mile House and eventually sold the saddle to William (Bill) Mackenzie, who lived on a ranch with his wife, Olive, in the 150 Mile – Rose Lake area. When Merv Furlong bought the ranch from Bill and Olive, he also got the saddle. It was Merv who donated it to the museum.

WHO USED IT? Lloyd "Cyclone" Smith, a competitive rodeo rider, used it.

Tell Me More

Lloyd "Cyclone" Smith was the famed King of the Cowboys at the Williams Lake Stampede. He was admired for his movie star looks and fearlessness. He won saddle and bareback competitions in both BC and Washington state.

Cariboo Chilcotin

› MUSEUM OF THE CARIBOO-CHILCOTIN

LLOYD "CYCLONE" SMITH'S SADDLE

Photo: Museum of the Cariboo-Chilcotin

WHY IS THE SADDLE IMPORTANT IN THIS AREA?

Photo: Museum of the Cariboo-Chilcotin

Lloyd "Cyclone" Smith is the only person who has ever died in the Williams Lake arena. During a stampede event in 1932, he was crushed underneath his horse as it collided with a runaway bronc. The Williams Lake Stampede is an important part of the city's history and culture. The first event was held in July 1919.

In the past, the rodeo brought together ranchers, cowboys, First Nations people and townsfolk all eager to hear the latest news and celebrate. There was something for everyone.

CONNECTIONS

Bonnie McCarroll was a famous champion rodeo performer and bronc rider in the United States in the 1920s. During this time, one-third of all rodeos featured women's competitive events. They rode as relay racers, trick riders and rough stock riders. This changed in 1929 when Bonnie had a terrible accident at the Pendleton Round-Up. She was thrown from her horse and dragged around the arena. Her foot had become trapped in the stirrup.

Bonnie McCarroll being thrown from Silver at the Pendleton Round-Up rodeo.
Photo: Wikimedia Commons, Walter S. Bowman.

Until this point, cowgirls in the rodeo were deeply admired for their strength and bravery, but the accident frightened people and drew attention to the dangers of the rodeo. Soon there was opposition to women competing in rough stock events. The rodeo promoters no longer wanted women competitors. Instead, they encouraged them to barrel race or become rodeo queens.

JUST THE FACTS

WILLIAMS LAKE BULL

WHAT IS IT? The Williams Lake Bull was used for the Throwing Bull competition, a stampede game originating in Williams Lake that made fun of politicians.

WHAT DOES IT LOOK LIKE? The bull is made out of an old gas drum. It's about the length of four footsteps belonging to a woman of average height. It looks like a carpenter's sawhorse made out of metal.

WHERE DOES IT COME FROM? It was a gift from the Williams Lake Stampede Association to the museum. In the 1950s, Williams Lake was the biggest shipper of bulls on the Pacific Great Eastern line of BC Rail, securing its reputation as a bona fide cowtown.

WHO USED IT? Jim Fraser, who was Williams Lake's mayor in the 1970s, loved to have fun with the city's reputation as a cowtown. He asked city and Williams Lake Stampede officials to find a family-friendly activity to be held at the 1972 stampede. The Throwing Bull was invented.

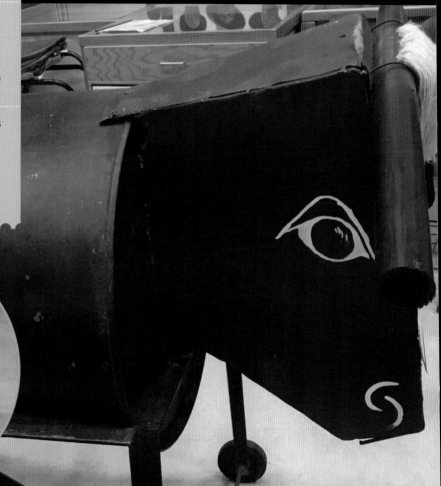

? WOULD YOU BELIEVE?

There's no record of who the stampede's official cow patty collector was, but it's known that one former mayor was in charge during his term. The cow patty collector was an important position as the patties had to be "cured until they were just right" according to the Williams Lake Tribune.

CONNECTIONS

In Pushkar, India, there's a camel fair that is a lot like the Williams Lake Stampede. It usually takes place in late October or early November. People come from all over India and the world to be there. The cultural events and competitions are very popular and include traditional dancing, tug-of-war (both men and women compete), a longest moustache competition, a bridal competition and camel races.

★ WHY IS THE WILLIAMS LAKE BULL IMPORTANT IN THIS AREA?

The bull attracted visitors and business to Williams Lake from all across Canada.

My Turn

Would you like to try your hand at throwing meadow muffins? Or, in this case, confetti bombs? Here's what you need: colourful construction paper, small paper bags, scissors and markers.

Start by making your confetti. You do this by cutting a piece of construction paper into pieces. Decorate your paper bag with your markers. Put the confetti into the paper bag. Before you do the next step, make sure to get permission. It can get messy. Blow up the bag. Now smack it hard and watch the confetti go flying.

Tell Me More

Williams Lake local Bernice Armstrong came up with the idea of the Throwing Bull. The contest worked like this: the bull's "body" (the gas drum) was filled with dried "meadow muffins" (cow manure). Participants (usually politicians) grabbed a muffin and tried to throw it as far as he or she could. It was trickier than you might think. Often the muffins fell apart as they were picked up or thrown. The participants were judged on distance, style, composure and – last but not least – their ability to persuade the judges they were indeed the best. The contest makes fun of the idea that politicians have a reputation for using a lot of "bull" (stretching the truth).

Additional rules included the following: competitors must successfully complete two throws, take at least one swig of "kick-a-poo" joy juice prior to selecting a meadow muffin and must not lick their fingers after the completion of each throw.

The Throwing Bull was used from 1972 to 1995. Nobody knows why it stopped being used. One theory is that as times have changed, so has our sense of humour.

COULD I WORK IN A MUSEUM?

NIKKI BOSE
Conservator, Okanagan Heritage Museum

You could be a conservator like Nikki Bose.

Here, Nikki talks about her job.

INTERVIEWER: What is your job?

NIKKI: If something is broken, I get to fix it. If it's dirty and needs cleaning, I figure out the best way to clean it. With conservation, you don't want to change the original object. Whatever I do needs to be reversible.

I'm a general objects conservator, but the big museums might have a **textile** conservator, a metals conservator or someone who just does works of art.

INTERVIEWER: Is being a conservator your only job at the museum?

NIKKI: My official title is **curator** of collections. As well as conservation, it **incorporates** being a registrar. Registrars deal with all donations coming in, all the objects out on loan, updating catalogue records, cataloguing new objects and finding items in storage that haven't been catalogued. Sometimes I also **deaccession** objects that no longer fit our collection, or maybe they are better suited at another museum. It's like streamlining the collection. The smaller the museum, the more hats you have to wear.

INTERVIEWER: Did you always want to be a conservator?

NIKKI: No, in high school I thought I was going to go into engineering. So, I took math and physics and chemistry. Halfway through the year, I wasn't loving it and I decided on **archaeology**. Digging in the dirt and finding stuff, travelling for work – that's what put me in the archaeology direction. Doing archaeology, finding stuff, I wondered, "How do you preserve it? How do you take care of these objects that have been in the ground for maybe thousands of years?"

INTERVIEWER: What **qualifications** do you need for this job?

NIKKI: Most museum jobs require formal museum training. I first studied archaeology in university. There are archaeological conservators and that's where I was hoping to end up. But those jobs are more rare than museum jobs. I also have a diploma in collections conservation and management.

For conservation, chemistry is very important because you need to know what materials are made of and how those materials are going to chemically react with their environment. For example, if I am doing a repair on an object, I need to make sure the adhesive I am using is going to be okay with it.

I need to know what is physically happening to the object, what is **degrading** or **corroding** the object. Why is it falling apart? Is it really falling apart, or does it just look bad?

If I know what is physically happening to it, I can stop it or slow it down. I'm not saying if you aren't good at chemistry you can't do this job, but it helps to have an interest or to understand the basics.

INTERVIEWER: What other skills do you need?

NIKKI: You have to have really good **dexterity**. The textiles I work on are all hand stitched. I use the "in and outs" that were done originally, so what I do can't be seen. Sometimes it can be quite tricky, and you need a lot of patience.

It's really good to be handy with tools, dental picks and **micro spatulas**. You have to be very organized, very methodical and calm. We work with a database called *Past Perfect*, which is used by museums, as well as Excel, Word and PowerPoint. I do a few workshops each year with the public, so that's public speaking.

It's also important to work well in a group setting. Everything that happens in a museum doesn't just affect you; it affects all the other departments. The exhibit team can't do what it does without talking to the collections team and without talking to programming. Programming needs to meet with events. They get objects from me. Knowing your strengths and weaknesses for group projects is important.

INTERVIEWER: What safety equipment do you work with?

NIKKI: The **fume hood** is super handy. I work with a lot of **solvents** like alcohol, acetone and mineral spirits. If an object is too big to put under the fume hood, I use a different air extraction unit. It's also called an elephant trunk because it kind of looks like one. [It works like a giant vacuum cleaner for air.]

I've got different masks, one for **particulates** and one for organic solvents, and eye protection.

The chest freezer is for pest infestations. This is how we deal with pests – we freeze them.

INTERVIEWER: What happens when things go wrong?

NIKKI: It happens. The more experience you have, the quicker you can see something going wrong and so the less damage occurs.

If I am going to wash paper, for example, I test all the inks for bleeding. But once I get the whole thing in water, if it starts to bleed, I have to be ready. I always assume things are going to go wrong, and I try to have a backup plan. How am I going to get the paper out of the water quickly? Do I have blotting paper ready? Do I have swabs so I can touch up certain areas?

Everyone makes mistakes. You have to take a deep breath; don't panic. Think, "What is happening? Why is it happening? How am I going to fix it?"

ALEXIS GAUVIN

Student Volunteer, Okanagan Science Centre

You could be a volunteer like Alexis Gauvin.

At the time this book was written, Alexis was a grade 12 student who started volunteering at the Okanagan Science Centre when she was in grade 11. Here, Alexis talks about her job.

INTERVIEWER: How did you hear about the volunteer opportunity?

ALEXIS: There was an announcement that said something like, "Are you wanting to make a difference and help out in a teen leadership group at the science centre?" and I was like, okay.

INTERVIEWER: What made you think you'd like to do this?

ALEXIS: I think mostly because I found out I really have a passion for science, and I'd like to get involved with it more. I knew science from the classroom, but I wanted to take it outside the classroom to see if I would still enjoy it.

INTERVIEWER: Had you been to the science centre before?

ALEXIS: I had been once with a school trip and that's it.

INTERVIEWER: Tell me a bit about the job.

ALEXIS: It entailed meeting as a group with some other teenagers and planning an event to attract more teenagers to the science centre.

INTERVIEWER: How many other students were there?

ALEXIS: Four.

INTERVIEWER: What skills did you need?

ALEXIS: First of all, it took a little courage to come out of my shell. At first, I asked one of my friends, "Hey would you like to do this with me?" and they weren't really interested. I realized I would have to do this on my own. I wasn't really afraid, but it was something that was slightly out of my comfort zone.

I'd say the skill I had to have was communication, because I really didn't know the other teenagers and you need to communicate your ideas with them. We had to get to know each other in a way that would help us understand each other. We also had to run an event ourselves.

INTERVIEWER: Working in a group and making everyone feel listened to can be tough.

ALEXIS: It is. Definitely. I remember at the beginning we didn't have a Teen Science Café [which is what we ended up doing] in mind. The idea was just to have a program, and we weren't quite sure yet what that was going to be. There were some people who wanted to make it a robotics club. But we thought that would be a lot less approachable for teens and our interest group would shrink. Another person wanted to do some sort of outdoor activity, designing something. One came up with game theory – we were going to run a camp with game theory because it comes down to a science – the chances of winning and losing. And then we figured the most approachable thing to do that would satisfy a broader audience would be the Teen Science Café.

INTERVIEWER: What activities did you organize?

ALEXIS: The first thing we brainstormed was spaghetti bridges because lots of teenagers enjoy that and I'm sure just about everyone has made one when they were a kid. You have hot glue and spaghetti. You have two tables placed with a gap in between and you see who can build the best bridge over the gap.

They got as much time as they wanted. Some people made triangles, some tried to make a bit of an arch, some people layered big spaghetti all together like beams. We tested them with water. We had a tie system that we put in the middle of the bridge, a tie that wouldn't damage the structure. And underneath was a pop bottle that we filled up with water and measured every time for the weight.

INTERVIEWER: Which structure won?

ALEXIS: It was the one with the most triangles.

INTERVIEWER: Were there other activities?

ALEXIS: We had what we called the egg carts. They had to package their egg however they liked, and they had wheels with axles so the egg could roll down a ramp. There was a ramp and a box at the end. The egg cart had to survive going down the ramp and hitting the end box without cracking. As the ramp got steeper, it got harder and harder to do. There were many who put wheels on four sides, top and bottom, so it would keep rolling.

The last thing we planned, but never got to, was a challenge to duct tape a person to the wall and see how long they would stay up. But we ran out of time.

INTERVIEWER: You then went on to work in a summer program at the science centre. Was it a paid position?

ALEXIS: Yes, it was a paid position. I never in a million years expected it to turn into a paid position, but it ended up that way. I had another job at the time. But I thought this would be a lot more "me" of a job to have. I would enjoy it a lot more than selling clothes. I thought that the science centre would give me more opportunity, and I always love spending time with kids. I coached kid's soccer in the past, so it really matched up well.

INTERVIEWER: Tell me about the job.

ALEXIS: There were nine one-week camps. Some camps were for grades 1 to 4, others for grades 5, 6 and 7. Most were for the younger group. We had many themes: myth busters, science and French; space odyssey; mad scientist, spies and private eyes; Lego robots (I didn't teach that one), cool girls, marine madness and master makers.

INTERVIEWER: Did you design the activities yourself?

ALEXIS: Mostly, but there was Kevin [Aschenmeier] who gave me suggestions for each theme. He gave me a starting point. Kevin is really amazing.

INTERVIEWER: Can you give me an example of some activities?

ALEXIS: For marine madness, I did different levels in the sea, different animals, like marine mammals and fish, and where sharks fit in because kids really like that. I also covered a little with ecosystems too. We looked at prehistoric marine life. I brought out some real fossils that we have and some copies of fossils that they were able to do some rubbings with, and I had them draw the fossils. They got to build their own prehistoric marine mammal. We talked about the characteristics – what you could see of the bones. I gave them Styrofoam balls and different paints and let their creativity run wild. It was quite a crafty camp.

INTERVIEWER: What about the older kids?

ALEXIS: They were more interested in making their own things. There was one activity that they really liked. It was the marble tracks. I gave them some marbles and materials like tubes and V-shaped cardboard that the marble could run through. And they built a track. At the end of the day they asked, "Can we please keep it up?" By the end of the week it was super complicated. The marble dropped into cones, funnelled down everywhere – it was amazing.

INTERVIEWER: Why would you encourage kids to get involved?

ALEXIS: It's the people. There are like-minded people there that you're almost sure to be instant friends with. I also enjoyed the learning aspect of it. It's in the culture of the science centre to be curious. I never had a limit put on me when it came to ideas for activities. I even came up with a new recipe for slime. It's a common activity, but we're not allowed to use borax anymore because it's a little bit dangerous around kids. So I searched the web and tried all these recipes and found one that worked. I bought some materials and tried it out. And I even failed one time. I thought the slime would work, but the saline solution that I bought was not the right kind. It didn't work out, but the kids had fun anyway. It was the last activity of the day and the parents came in and said, "What is this?" I said, "It's an experiment." I tried it with them the next day and it worked out well. I bought the right kind of saline. We still make the slime. It's a common activity and we use the slime recipe that I tested out and I'm really proud of that.

INTERVIEWER: Will you do another Teen Science Café?

ALEXIS: Yes. There will be new activities for sure. We have one new girl who has joined, so we'll see if she brings any cool ideas to the table, and I'm really excited to see where it goes.

CORALEE MILLER
Museum Assistant,
Snсəwips Heritage Museum

You could be a **museum assistant** like Coralee Miller.

Here, Coralee talks about her job.

INTERVIEWER: What is your job?

CORALEE: My job is a bit of everything. I deal with the daily maintenance of the museum. I dust the exhibits, I put them up and I take them down. I help with the planning process and I talk to guests when they come in. I let them know about the stories. I tour them through and give them the context for what they're looking at.

INTERVIEWER: What did you study?

CORALEE: It was actually funny. I never ever thought I'd be in a museum. I was actually an art student. I'm working toward my Bachelor of Fine Arts. And that comes in handy when you're creating a story, and when you're making an exhibit. You have to know what colours work best and how to direct the gaze of the visitor. Lighting is important and you learn how to set the space so it's more visually appealing.

INTERVIEWER: What do you love about museums?

CORALEE: What I love is learning about the life an object had before it made it to the museum. It wasn't made to go into a museum. Someone had this item; they loved it; they used it. It had a life and now it's here.

Whenever we get an item, there's a bit of detective work that comes with it. What year did it come from? What was happening during that time? What kind of particular person had the item? From there, we learn the story.

INTERVIEWER: What kind of person do you think you need to be to work in a museum?

CORALEE: I think the best kind of person to work in a museum is someone who is curious. Someone who likes to visit with the piece and get to know it. Someone who works in a museum should be kind – you have a lot of people visiting, so you have to be able to provide them with that story. A good sense of humour helps.

INTERVIEWER: What is your favourite belonging in your museum?

CORALEE: My museum? My favourite piece is the cradleboard that belongs to my little cousin. [Learn about this piece on page 38.] I love the culture around it. We took our kids everywhere.

INTERVIEWER: What is one thing people may not know about working in a museum?

CORALEE: Working in a museum can be stressful when there's not enough storage and a lot of artifacts.

INTERVIEWER: Is there something people should know about museums?

CORALEE: A lot of people think museums are boring, but I think museums are trying very hard to modernize, to be more accessible to the younger generations. And so, right now, museums are working hard to implement more technological advances, so more interactive maps, more video, documentaries.

I think that we just have to get back to going to museums. It's a great way to get in touch with your community. We need to inspire that curiosity of *where am I living right now – and how did we live? What are people working toward now?* But that's the different thing about our museum; we don't only place focus on the past, we're still making history today because we're not supposed to be alive.

It's a neat thing to think about how we're making history right now. I'm guessing in another 100 years, kids are going to be in a museum and they're going to be saying "LOL MP3s."

INTERVIEWER: One piece of advice for a kid who wants to work in a museum.

CORALEE: Be brave. If you're a shy person as I was, I was very shy – I hated public speaking. But I saw my boss doing tours, and I felt that I wanted to pull my weight too, and so I learned everything I could about the collection pieces, and pretty soon I was running the tours. So I feel like museum work helps me become closer to my community, helps me engage with new people and boosts my confidence.

AFTERWORD

Now that you've read this book, you will know a great many things about museums.

You will know that museums are located in all sorts of places and aren't just in big cities. They remind us of the good and the bad things that have happened in our communities. They serve as a warning that some mistakes should never be repeated. In this way, museums help us create better futures.

You will know that great museums come in a variety of shapes and sizes. And what matters is not whether a museum is big or small, it's that they are open to all. Everyone is welcome: kids, seniors, people of different cultures and genders. At the museum, everyone will find something they can connect with.

You know that a belonging in a museum doesn't have to cost a lot of money, be old or rare. It doesn't even have to stay at the museum all the time. Museum belongings are about stories, and not just about famous people but normal people like me, and you, your parents, your grandparents and even your great-great-great-grandparents.

You will know that belongings make their way to museums in many different ways. Some belongings are donated by people in the community, while others are just on loan. You can visit the same museum over and over and notice something new each time. It's like visiting a good friend you like hanging out with. Each time you visit, you see another part of them.

Now that you know a little more, we want you to tell us something. If you started a museum, what would you put in it? Where would it be? Would it be small or big? What would you fill it with? What would you want people to know about where you live, how you spend your time and about your community? What stories would you share with the kids of the future?

Think about it.

ACKNOWLEDGEMENTS

The authors gratefully acknowledge the contributions of the following people to this book: Kathy Paulos, Ashcroft Museum; Deborah Chapman, R. J. Haney Heritage Village & Museum; Carla-Jean Stokes, Historic O'Keefe Ranch and Interior Heritage Society; Carson Albrecht, Kevin Aschenmeier, Alexis Gauvin, Okanagan Science Centre; Amanda Snyder, Tara Hurley, Nikki Bose, Okanagan Heritage Museum; Danielle Heavy Head, Blackfoot Digital Library Liaison, University of Lethbridge.

Thank you to the staff of the Sncəwips Heritage Museum for providing their knowledge and sharing their heritage and culture: Jordan Coble, Coralee Miller and Krystal Lezard.

Thank you to Julien Butler, Summerland Museum and Archives Society; Dennis Oomen, Penticton Museum & Archives; Todd Davidson, Princeton & District Museum & Archives; Julianna Weisgarber, Veronica Parkes, Oliver & District Heritage Society Museum; Cathy English, Revelstoke Museum & Archives; Honor Neve and staff, Cranbrook History Centre; and Margaret Teneese, archivist, Ktunaxa Nation Council.

Thank you to Doreen MacLean, president of the Greenwood Heritage Society and the visitor centre manager, and Greenwood Heritage Society treasurer and long-time volunteer, Clare Folvik. Clare's family was interned in Greenwood in 1942. She manages a museum database of the Japanese Canadian families that were interned in Greenwood.

Thank you to Jessica Van Oostwaard, Fort Steele Heritage Town; Tammy Bradford and staff, The Creston Museum and Archives; Debbie McIntosh, Andrea Ryman, Castlegar Station Museum; Catherine Allaway, Theresa Tremaine, Nikkei Internment Memorial Centre; Lisa Uyeda, Linda Kawamoto Reid, Nikkei National Museum and Cultural Centre; Astrid Heyerdahl, J. P. Stienne, Indigenous educator Lesley Garlow, Anna Purcell, Touchstones Nelson: Museum of Art and History; Joelle Hodgins, Sara Wright and staff, Rossland Museum & Discovery Centre; Museum & Heritage Manager for the City of Quesnel Elizabeth Hunter, Quesnel & District Museum and Archives; Mary Telfer, the director of the Museum of the Cariboo-Chilcotin Society's board of directors and the former vice-president, and Alex Geris, Museum of the Cariboo-Chilcotin.

GLOSSARY

amenities: Something that makes life more pleasant, like dishwashers, microwaves and refrigerators.

archaeology: The study of human history by digging up sites and studying objects found there.

archive: A collection of historical records.

artifact: Something made by humans that has a historical or cultural interest.

awl: A small pointed tool for creating holes in things.

axle: A long rod on which wheels are attached.

bias: An opinion held by someone without giving an equal chance to another idea.

bicorn: A style of hat that has two corners of its brim drawn together.

biologist: Someone who has special knowledge of living creatures.

biotope: Another word for habitat.

braiding: Decoration on a piece of clothing that is made of metal or metallic thread.

bunker: Usually underground rooms designed to protect people from bombs or other attacks.

Canada Border Services Agency: Works to help the movement of certified travellers and authorized trade.

cenotaph: A marker or an empty tomb put up in tribute to a group of people whose remains are somewhere else.

civil war: A war between two groups from one country but with different beliefs.

claim: A square or rectangular area of Crown land miners measure out. When they register this land, they are allowed to mine or prospect on that land.

Cold War: A time in history between 1947 and 1991 when there was tension between the United States and the Soviet Union.

conquistador: The Spanish word for conqueror.

corroding: Eating away at.

curator: Someone who looks after the belongings of a collection, or gallery or museum.

customs office: An office where taxes are collected on products coming into the country.

deaccession: Remove officially.

decontamination: A way to clean people or objects that have been exposed to hazardous or dangerous materials.

degrading: Breaking down.

descendant: A plant or animal related to a specific plant or animal that lived long ago.

dexterity: Being skilled with your hands.

diorama: A three-dimensional model, either miniature or full size.

ecosystem: A community of plants and animals and where they live.

embossed: A design on an object that stands out or is raised.

expropriated: When the government takes property from a landowner.

fallout: In the case of nuclear war, radioactive particles that fall out of the sky.

fossil: The remains, or the cast of an animal, plant or a single cell life form that existed in a time before written record.

fume hood: A place where scientists can work with toxic fumes and dust. An exhaust fan (like the one over your stove) pulls the fumes and dust out of the enclosure.

functional: Something designed to be useful.

geographical: The physical markings of an area of land.

geologist: An expert on the earth and its makeup, matter, history and the things that affect it.

ghost town: A town where either nobody or very few people live anymore.

gorge: A narrow valley between hills or mountains with steep rocky sides.

Great War: A war also called the First World War. It began in Europe in 1914 and ended in 1918. One of the largest wars in history.

heritage: Habits and customs that are passed down from one generation of family to the next.

heyday: A time in history when a person, place or thing had its greatest success.

hibernacula: A place where a creature can hide and feel safe, like a fox's den.

homage: An expression of respect.

hopper: A container holding (in this case) soya beans that are fed into the grinder.

incorporates: Includes.

infantry: A foot soldier.

internment: Being held as a prisoner for political or military reasons.

Jurassic: A period in Earth's life that took place between 144 and 180 million years ago.

kimono: A traditional Japanese piece of clothing worn by men and women.

labour camps: Places where people are forced to live and do work as a kind of punishment. How the inmates of these camps are treated depends on those running the camps.

latitudes: Along with longitudes, these are lines that cover Earth with a grid. This grid marks the location of places all across the world.

ledger: A book detailing financial accounts.

legacy: Knowledge received from an ancestor.

liaison: Communication or cooperation.

mandate: A rule or a particular way of doing something.

micro spatula: A tool used in a laboratory for flipping things or spreading substances.

microfilm: Film that contains tiny photographs of printed material like books and newspapers.

misalignment: Being out of the correct position.

mortar: A bowl made of hard material in which ingredients are ground.

natural habitat: An area where a specific creature feels comfortable living.

Nikkei: A term used in Japan to refer to people of Japanese ancestry who are living abroad as citizens of other countries.

nomadic: Not having a permanent home; roaming from place to place.

nonvenomous: Not poisonous.

nymph: A female mythological creature from Greek and Roman mythology.

paleontologist: A person who studies fossils.

papyrus: Paper made from reeds in ancient Egypt.

particulates: Small solid or liquid particles like dust.

patent: An agreement that stops people from using something an inventor has created without paying the inventor.

perishables: Food not likely to stay fresh for long if not eaten quickly or not used.

perspective: A method used by artists to make flat objects look three-dimensional or real; the way you see something that is different from the way other people see something.

planetarium: A domed theatre on which a picture of the night sky is projected.

pneumatic: Describes equipment that is powered by compressed air.

qualifications: Experience, training or schooling required for a job.

rasp: A coarse or rough file.

replica: A copy of an object or building.

savoury: Refers to a taste that isn't sweet.

scabbard: A casing for a blade of a sword or dagger.

sedimentary: When sand, mud and pebbles get squished together over time and turn to rock.

sibling: A brother or sister.

skip: A metal car or wagon used in a mine to move ore, people or equipment.

solvents: Usually a liquid used to dissolve things.

species: A way to describe a group of animals, plants and living things that can breed with each other.

specimen: An example of a species used for study.

suture: Stitches used to hold together the edges of a wound or cut.

tabloid: Often meaning a newspaper that reports sensational (sometimes exaggerated or untrue) stories.

teletype: A machine used in the early to mid-20th century to transmit typed messages over wires or radio waves.

textile: Another word for fabric or material.

tourniquet: Cord or bandage used to stop the flow of blood through the veins.

tuberculosis: A dangerous disease that attacks the lungs.

typesetter: Before computers and digital printers, the words of a text were set in metal type and then printed on a printing press.

War Measures Act: A special rule that gives the government extra powers during an emergency. This act, if used badly, can be very dangerous as it gives the government the right to jail and arrest people without a trial or even a reason.

yak: A cousin of the cow. It has long handlebar horns.

SELECTED SOURCES

THOMPSON/OKANAGAN
ASHCROFT MUSEUM

Telephone Exchange

"Telephone Exchange." *Wikipedia*. https://en.wikipedia.org/wiki/Telephone_exchange.

Horse Fly Net

Jurga, Fran. "The Humane Thing To Do: When Horse Blankets Were the Law." *EQUUS*. https://equusmagazine.com/blog-equus/horse-blankets-law-humane-history-55156.

Tomato Knife

"A Tax on the Love Apple." *Four String Farm*. https://fourstringfarm.com/tag/history-of-tomato/.

R. J. HANEY HERITAGE VILLAGE & MUSEUM

Fire Bucket

"Crassus' Fire Brigade." *Imperium Romanum*. https://www.imperiumromanum.edu.pl/en/curiosities/crassus-fire-brigade/.

School Slate

Chavannes, Edouard. "Chinese Books before the Invention of Paper." https://opensiuc.lib.siu.edu/cgi/viewcontent.cgi?article=2053&context=ocj.

Cossins, Daniel. "We Thought the Incas Couldn't Write. These Knots Change Everything." *New Scientist*. https://www.newscientist.com/article/mg23931972-600-we-thought-the-incas-couldnt-write-these-knots-change-everything/.

HISTORIC O'KEEFE RANCH

Butter Churn

"Butter Is as Old as History." *Butter through the Ages*. http://www.webexhibits.org/butter/history-intro.html.

Kreutzweiser, Erwin. "Margarine." *The Canadian Encyclopedia*. https://www.thecanadianencyclopedia.ca/en/article/margarine.

"Scrumptious Science: Shaking Up Butter." *Scientific American*. https://www.scientificamerican.com/article/bring-science-home-shaking-butter/.

Painting of an English Gentleman

Clark, Josh. "Why Do the Eyes in Paintings Seem to Follow You Sometimes?" *How Stuff Works*. https://entertainment.howstuffworks.com/arts/artwork/eyes-in-painting-follow.htm.

Sample, Ian. "How the Laughing Cavalier Keeps an Eye on Everybody." *The Guardian*. https://www.theguardian.com/science/2004/sep/22/arts.science.

OKANAGAN SCIENCE CENTRE

Gyro Chair

"Bull-Leaping: The Modern Sport of Course Landaise Offers Ethnoarchaeologists Clues about the Ancient Tradition of Bull-Leaping." *National Geographic Society*. https://www.nationalgeographic.org/media/bull-leaping/.

Bruce Aikenhead Planetarium

"The Gottorp (Great Academic) Globe." *Kunstkamera*. http://www.kunstkamera.ru/en/museum/kunst_hist/5/5_3.

Bitey McBiteface the Piranha

Haynes Steward, Julian. *Handbook of South American Indians*. Smithsonian Institution Bureau of American Ethnology Bulletin 143. Washington, DC: Government Printing Office, 1946. https://books.google.ca.

OKANAGAN HERITAGE MUSEUM

Grizzly Bear

"Grizzly Bear Facts." *Animal Facts Encyclopedia*. https://www.animalfactsencyclopedia.com/Grizzly-bear-facts.html.

Wright, William H. *The Grizzly Bear: The Narrative of a Hunter-Naturalist*. Lincoln: University of Nebraska Press, 1977. https://books.google.ca.

Millstone

"Metate and Mano." *Gourmet Sleuth*. https://www.gourmetsleuth.com/articles/detail/metate-y-mano.

Beaver Skeleton

Heavy Head, Adrienne Danielle, and Mary Greenshields. "Let Me Draw You a Map: Knowledge Management from 'Two Completely Different Streams of Thought.'" *Canadian Journal of Academic Librarianship*. https://cjal.ca/index.php/capal/article/view/31467.

SNCƏWIPS HERITAGE MUSEUM

Fishing Weir/nsyilxcɔ: sxʷlikn

Hirst, K. Kris. "All About the Fish Weir." *ThoughtCo*, January 26, 2018. https://www.thoughtco.com/fish-weir-ancient-fishing-tool-170925.

Najihah, Aina. "This Amazing Japanese Fish Trap Only Uses Bamboo But It Is Far More Effective than a Fishing Rod or a Net." *GoodTimes*, May 2, 2018. http://en.goodtimes.my/2018/05/02/this-amazing-japanese-fish-trap-only-uses-bamboo-but-it-is-far-more-effective-than-a-fishing-rod-or-a-net/.

"Pacific Willow." *BC Living, Canada Wide Media Limited*, September 1, 2004. https://www.bcliving.ca/pacific-willow.

Cradleboard/nsyilxcɔ Mx̌ʷal-

Alsgaard, Asia. "Reviving Tradition: One Cradleboard at a Time." *Cultural Survival*, March 24, 2015. https://www.culturalsurvival.org/news/reviving-tradition-one-cradleboard-time.

SUMMERLAND MUSEUM AND ARCHIVES SOCIETY

Tent House

Ott, Sherry. "What Is a Mongolian Ger and Traditions?" *Ott's World*, September 30, 2011. https://www.ottsworld.com/blogs/mongolian-gers/.

Velocipede

"The Velocipede." *Age of Revolution: Making the World Over.* https://ageofrevolution.org/200-object/velocipede/.

"Velocipede." *Wikipedia.* https://en.wikipedia.org/wiki/Velocipede.

Kettle Valley Station

"About Us, a Brief History." *The Kettle Valley Steam Railway.* https://www.kettlevalleyrail.org/about/.

Arendt, John. "Historian to Speak about Steam Railway's Past." *Summerland Review*, March 29, 2019. https://www.summerlandreview.com/news/historian-to-speak-about-steam-railways-past/.

"Countries without a Railway Network." *World Atlas.* https://www.worldatlas.com/articles/countries-without-a-railway-network.html.

"The Kettle Valley Railway, Okanagan History Vignette." *En Copain.* http://en.copian.ca/library/learning/okanagan/history/2railway.pdf.

"Portraits, Mary Gordon Blewett, Family Histories." *Summerland Museum.* https://static1.squarespace.com/static/5995f4e96b8f5b9ef7c7355f/t/5d13a93b5891ab0001e8b044/1561569808870/30-Family+Histories+Vol.+3.pdf.

PENTICTON MUSEUM & ARCHIVES

Penny Farthing

"Penny Farthing." *Wikipedia.* https://en.wikipedia.org/wiki/Penny-farthing.

"Penny Farthing: Facts and Information." *Primary Facts.* https://primaryfacts.com/4785/penny-farthing-facts-and-information/.

Thorpe, J. R. "The Feminist History of Bicycles." *Bustle*, May 12, 2017. https://www.bustle.com/p/the-feminist-history-of-bicycles-57455.

Private Kenyon's Sweater

Boyd, Dale. "Remembrance Day: Penticton's Prisoner of War." *Penticton Western News*, November 11, 2016. https://www.pentictonwesternnews.com/news/remembrance-day-pentictons-prisoner-of-war/.

Carter, David J. "Prisoner of War Camps in Canada." *The Canadian Encyclopedia.* https://www.thecanadianencyclopedia.ca/en/article/prisoner-of-war-camps-in-canada.

Royde-Smith, John Graham, and Dennis E. Showalter. "World War I, 1914 – 1918." *Encyclopedia Britannica.* https://www.britannica.com/event/World-War-I.

Great Basin Gopher Snake

Cartwright, Mark. "Asclepius." *Ancient History Encyclopedia.* https://www.ancient.eu/Asclepius/.

"The Reptiles of British Colombia: Great Basin Gopher Snake." Thompson Rivers University and British Colombia Ministry of the Environment. https://www.bcreptiles.ca/snakes/grtbasingopher.htm.

"Rod of Asclepius." *Wikipedia.* https://en.wikipedia.org/wiki/Rod_of_Asclepius.

Vennesland, Ross. "Species Ranking in British Columbia." BC Conservation Data Centre, March 2002. http://www.env.gov.bc.ca/wld/documents/ranking.pdf.

PRINCETON & DISTRICT MUSEUM & ARCHIVES

Ice Plow

Eschner, Kat. "The First Artificial Skating Rinks Looked Pretty but Smelled Terrible." *Smithsonian Magazine*, June 2, 2017. https://www.smithsonianmag.com/smart-news/first-artificial-skating-rinks-looked-pretty-smelled-terrible-180963486.

Scorpionfly Fossil

Bains, Camille. "Scorpionfly Discovery Highlights Prehistoric Link between Canada and Russia." *The Canadian Press*, April 4, 2018. https://www.cbc.ca/news/canada/british-columbia/b-c-russia-scorpionfly-connection-1.4604551.

Black, Riley. "Meet Chilesaurus, a New Raptor-Like Dinosaur with a Vegetarian Diet." *Smithsonian Magazine*, April 27, 2015. https://www.smithsonianmag.com/science-nature/meet-chilesaurus-new-raptor-dinosaur-vegetarian-diet-180955101/.

The Canadian Press. "53 Million Year Old Scorpionfly Fossil Found in BC." *The Similkameen Spotlight*, April 3, 2018. https://www.similkameenspotlight.com/national-news/53-million-year-old-scorpionfly-fossil-found-in-b-c/.

Stephenson, Kirsten. "Kid Makes History after Discovering Fossil of Unknown Dinosaur Species in Chile." *Guinness World Records*, January 31, 2018. https://www.guinnessworldrecords.com/news/2018/1/kid-makes-history-after-discovering-fossil-of-unknown-dinosaur-species-in-chile-512385/.

Civil War Sword

"Civil War Facts, American Battlefield Trust." *American Battlefield Trust*. https://www.google.com/search?client=safari&rls=en&q=american+civil+war+deaths+total&ie=UTF-8&oe=UTF-8.

"History of the American Civil War." *Civil War*. http://www.civilwar.com/history/soldier-life-85851/148551-leisure-activities-during-the-civil-war.html.

Okanagan Historical Society Report, "Myths & Legends – General Sherman's Sword." *Princeton & District Museum & Archives News*, No. 37, November 1, 1973. https://www.princetonmuseum.org/uploads/1/0/9/5/109517281/newsletter_aug_sep_oct_18.pdf.

OLIVER & DISTRICT HERITAGE SOCIETY MUSEUM

Apple Packing Table

"Simply, A History of the Apple." *New Internationalist*, October 5, 1990. https://newint.org/features/1990/10/05/simply.

Kangaroo Platform

"Banana Production Guide." *Pinoy Bisnes Ideas*, July 21, 2016. https://www.pinoybisnes.com/agri-business/banana-production-guide/.

"Bananas: Their History, Cultivation and Production." *Facts and Details*. http://factsanddetails.com/world/cat54/sub343/item1577.html.

Fairview Jail

Cancela, Julie. "Fairview." *Osoyoos and District Museum and Archives*, 1986. http://osoyoosmuseum.ca/index.php/about-us/history-of-osoyoos/mining/34-about/history-of-osoyoos/mining/the-gold-rush/69-the-mines-at-fairview.html.

Lacy, Rogyn. "Curious Canadian Cemeteries: Fairview Cemetery, Oliver, British Columbia." *Spade & the Grave*, January 9, 2019. https://spadeandthegrave.com/2019/01/09/curious-canadian-cemeteries-fairview-cemetery-oliver-british-columbia/.

Rossiter, Philip. "Work in the Mines." *Okanagan Historical Report*. http://osoyoosmuseum.ca/index.php/about-us/history-of-osoyoos/mining/34-about/history-of-osoyoos/mining/the-gold-rush/69-the-mines-at-fairview.html.

"Slang Words for Jail." *Love to Know Corp.* https://grammar.yourdictionary.com/slang/slang-words-for-jail.html.

White, Hester E. "A Name as Fair as the View." *Okanagan Historical Report,* No. 12, 1948. http://osoyoosmuseum.ca/index.php/about-us/history-of-osoyoos/mining/34-about/history-of-osoyoos/mining/the-gold-rush/69-the-mines-at-fairview.html.

REVELSTOKE MUSEUM & ARCHIVES

Packsaddle
"The Plains People: Transportation." *Canada's First Peoples*. https://firstpeoplesofcanada.com/fp_groups/fp_plains4.html.

Fur Press
"Siberian Fur Trade." *Wikipedia*. https://en.wikipedia.org/wiki/Siberian_fur_trade.

Poison Bottle
"Antique Poison Bottles." *Collectors Weekly*. https://www.collectorsweekly.com/bottles/poison-bottles.

GREENWOOD MUSEUM & VISITOR CENTRE

Replica of Room Used by a Japanese Canadian Family during Their Internment
Saylors, Kathleen. "Greenwood Recognizes Internment Sites with Historic Signs." *Boundary Creek Times*, October 19, 2018. https://www.boundarycreektimes.com/news/greenwood-recognizes-internment-sites-with-historic-signs/.

Tasaka, Chuck. "Greenwood, BC: First Internment Center." *Japanese American National Museum*, January 29, 2016. http://www.discovernikkei.org/en/journal/2016/1/29/greenwood.

Porcelain Sculpture of the Three Graces
Ludwig, Michaela. "10 British Columbia Ghost Towns Forgotten by Time." *Canadian Traveller*, March 26, 2015. https://www.canadiantraveller.com/10_British_Columbia_Ghost_Towns_Forgotten_By_Time.

"Tales beyond Belief." *Siteseen Ltd.* http://www.talesbeyondbelief.com/nymphs/three-graces.htm.

Colin "Scott" McRae's Violin
"Chanter." *Wikipedia*. https://en.wikipedia.org/wiki/Chanter.

"Fiddle vs. Violin: Are Violins and Fiddles Different?" *Johnson String Instrument*. https://www.johnsonstring.com/violins-facts/fiddle-vs-violin.htm.

Lederman, Anne, and Christina Smith. "Fiddling." *The Canadian Encyclopedia*. https://thecanadianencyclopedia.ca/en/article/fiddling-emc.

Smith Hill, Pamela. "Pa's Fiddle: Now Is Now." *Little House on the Prairie*, December 12, 2014. http://littlehouseontheprairie.com/pas-fiddle-now-is-now/.

KOOTENAY/ROCKY MOUNTAINS
CRANBROOK HISTORY CENTRE

Stuffed Toy Panda Bear

"The History of Steiff Teddy Bears: A Timeline for Margarete Steiff, and Her Beloved Bears." *Steiff*. https://www.steiffteddybears.co.uk/more-things-steiff/history-of-steiff-bears.php.

Trilobite

"The Strangest Trilobites." *American Museum of Natural History*. https://www.amnh.org/research/paleontology/collections/fossil-invertebrate-collection/trilobite-website/the-trilobite-files/the-strangest-trilobites.

Surgical Kit

"About Us." *Médecins Sans Frontières/Doctors Without Borders*. https://www.doctorswithoutborders.ca/content/about-us.

FORT STEELE HERITAGE TOWN

Trephine Surgical Tool

Wade, Lizzie. "South America's Inca Civilization Was Better at Skull Surgery than Civil War Doctors." *Science*. https://www.sciencemag.org/news/2018/06/south-america-s-inca-civilization-was-better-skull-surgery-civil-war-doctors.

Wylie, Robin. "Why Our Ancestors Drilled Holes in Each Other's Skulls." *BBC*. http://www.bbc.com/earth/story/20160826-why-our-ancestors-drilled-holes-in-each-others-skulls.

The Herb Hawkins Locomotive #1077

Bracken, Joe. "Historic Trains #1077 at Fort Steele." *Canadian Heartland Training Railway*. http://chtr.ca/historic-trains-1077-at-fort-steele/.

Turner, Robert D. "Logging Railroads and Locomotives in British Columbia: A Background Summary and the Preservation Record." *Material Culture Review*. https://journals.lib.unb.ca/index.php/MCR/article/view/17066/22908.

Sidesaddle

Johnson, Ben. "Riding Side-Saddle." *Historic UK*. https://www.historic-uk.com/CultureUK/Riding-SideSaddle/.

Walsh, Bob. "Walcha History: Esther Stace the Fearless Horsewoman." *Walcha News*. https://www.walchanewsonline.com.au/story/5270137/side-saddle-legend/.

THE CRESTON MUSEUM AND ARCHIVES

TRS-80 Model III Computer

"TRS-80." *Wikipedia*. https://en.wikipedia.org/wiki/TRS-80.

Logging Arch

"The Outstanding Megalithic Necropolis That Is the Tumulus of Bougon." *Ancient Origins: Reconstructing the Story of Humanity's Past*. https://www.ancient-origins.net/users/dhwty.

230th Forestry Battalion: Service Medals, Paybooks and Sergeant's Stripes

McKelvey, Peter. "New Zealand Foresters at War." *NZ Journal of Forestry*. http://nzjf.org.nz/free_issues/NZJF45_4_2001/A0695568-D535-44BE-9369-CD61A0303A06.pdf.

TOUCHSTONES NELSON: MUSEUM OF ART AND HISTORY

Edgar Dewdney's Lieutenant-Governor's Uniform

"Canada Declared the Sinixt Extinct. But the Sinixt Say They Are Alive and Well." *The Doc Project*, January 20, 2020. https://www.cbc.ca/radio/docproject/canada-declared-the-sinixt-extinct-but-the-sinixt-say-they-are-alive-and-well-1.5428244.

"History of Castlegar up to 1873." https://www.castlegar.ca/visitors/about-castlegar/history/.

Innes, Robert Alexander. "Clearing the Plains of Accountability." *Shekon Neechie: An Indigenous History Site*. June 21, 2018. https://shekonneechie.ca/2018/06/21/clearing-the-plains-of-accountability/.

Kassam, Ashifa. "Sinixt First Nation Wins Recognition in Canada Decades after 'Extinction.'" *The Guardian*, March 30, 2017. https://www.theguardian.com/world/2017/mar/30/canada-sinixt-first-nation-extinct-recognition.

Titley, Brian. "Dewdney, Edgar (1835 – 1916)." *Indigenous Saskatchewan Encyclopedia*, University of Saskatchewan. https://teaching.usask.ca/indigenoussk/import/dewdney_edgar_1835-1916.php.

Wilkinson, Myler, and Duff Sutherland. "'From Our Side We Will Be Good Neighbour[s] to Them': Doukhobor – Sinixt Relations at the Confluence of the Kootenay and Columbia Rivers in the Early Twentieth Century." *BC Studies*, Summer 2012. https://ojs.library.ubc.ca/index.php/bcstudies/article/view/2380.

1950s Nuclear Bomb Shelter

Peters, Dave. "The Diefenbunker – Cold War Secret Defence Facility." *Mysteries of Canada*. https://www.mysteriesofcanada.com/military/diefenbunker/.

CASTLEGAR STATION MUSEUM

Diving Suit

"The Progression of the Diving Suit." *Dive Centre Bahamas*. https://www.scubadivebahamas.com/the-progression-of-the-diving-suit/.

Portable Electrohome Record Player

Riley, Saron. "Record Players Were the Infotainment Systems of the 1950s and '60s: Early Adventures in Mobile Fidelity." *Consumer Reports*. https://www.consumerreports.org/cro/news/2014/04/record-players-were-the-infotainment-systems-of-the-1950s-and-60s/index.htm.

NIKKEI INTERNMENT MEMORIAL CENTRE

Geta

Halbout, Nataliya. "Pattens." *Fashion History Timeline*. https://fashionhistory.fitnyc.edu/pattens/.

"Mickey Mouse Geta (Japanese Sandals)." *50 Objects*. https://50objects.org/object/mickey-mouse-geta-japanese-sandals/.

Mochi Mallet

Maikawa, Frank. "The Evolution of a Canadian 'Enemy Alien' – The Frank Maikawa Story," Part 8 of 12. *Discover Nikkei*. http://www.discovernikkei.org/en/journal/2013/4/24/4779/.

"Pounded Yam." *All Nigerian Foods*. https://allnigerianfoods.com/pounded-yam.

Truefaith7. "The Moon Rabbit in Legend and Culture." *Owlcation*. https://owlcation.com/social-sciences/moon-rabbit.

ROSSLAND MUSEUM & DISCOVERY CENTRE

Red Mountain Chairlift

Engber, Daniel. "Who Made That Ski Lift?" *The New York Times*. https://www.nytimes.com/2014/02/23/magazine/who-made-that-ski-lift.html.

Father Pat Memorial Ambulance

"History." *Flying Doctor*. https://www.flyingdoctor.org.au/about-the-rfds/history/.

"Royal Flying Doctor Service of Australia." *Wikipedia*. https://en.wikipedia.org/wiki/Royal_Flying_Doctor_Service_of_Australia.

CARIBOO CHILCOTIN
QUESNEL & DISTRICT MUSEUM AND ARCHIVES

Royal Bank Bathtub

"5 Things to Know about a Clawfoot Tub." *Boston Standard*, August 21, 2013. https://www.bostonstandardplumbing.com/blog/5-things-to-know-about-a-clawfoot-tub/.

"History: A Legacy in the Making." *Kohler New Zealand Ltd*. https://kohler.co.nz/about-us/History.html.

"If You Took a Bath Today, Thank a Pig." *Year Struck*. https://year-struck.com/2012/04/15/if-you-took-a-bath-today-thank-a-pig/.

Spellen, Suzanne (aka Montrose Morris). "From Pakistan to Brooklyn: A Quick History of the Bathroom." *Brownstoner*, November 28, 2016. https://www.brownstoner.com/architecture/victorian-bathroom-history-plumbing-brooklyn-architecture-interiors/.

Inaugural RCMP Turban

Baker, Rafferty. "As He Readies for New Role, 1st Mountie to Wear Turban Reflects on RCMP career." *CBC News*, August 5, 2019. https://www.cbc.ca/news/canada/british-columbia/baltej-dhillon-1st-turban-wearing-rcmp-officer-retires-1.5233535.

Foot, Richard. "Baltej Dhillon Case." *The Canadian Encyclopedia*, April 6, 2019. https://www.thecanadianencyclopedia.ca/en/article/baltej-dhillon-case.

Kite, Mary, and Bernard E. Whitley, Jr. "Breaking Prejudice, Language Activity." Virginia Ball Center for Creative Inquiry, Ball State University. http://breakingprejudice.org/teaching/group-activities/language-activity/.

"Racism." *Kids Net Encyclopedia*. http://encyclopedia.kids.net.au/page/ra/Racism.

"Reflection Activity: Identity." *Teaching Tolerance Magazine*. https://www.tolerance.org/professional-development/reflection-activity-identity.

"The Turban That Rocked the RCMP: How Baltej Singh Dhillon Challenged the RCMP – and Won." *CBC Radio*, May 11, 2017. https://www.cbc.ca/2017/canadathestoryofus/the-turban-that-rocked-the-rcmp-how-baltej-singh-dhillon-challenged-the-rcmp-and-won-1.4110271.

"What Is the Significance of the Turban?" *World Sikh Organization of Canada*. http://www.worldsikh.org/what_is_the_significance_of_the_turban.

Family Portrait by C. S. Wing

"Upstairs at Wah Lee's: Portraits from the C. S. Wing Studio." *The Courtenay and District Museum.* https://www.courtenaymuseum.ca/programmes-exhibits/online-exhibits/upstairs-at-wah-lees-portraits-from-the-c-s-wing-studio/.

"Upstairs at Wah Lee's: Portraits from the C. S. Wing Studio." *The Royal BC Museum.* https://royalbcmuseum.bc.ca/assets/2008-09-16-Wah-Lee-Portraits-Fast-Facts.pdf.

MUSEUM OF THE CARIBOO-CHILCOTIN

Dr. Bothamley's Dentist Chair and Tool Stand

"The Mysteries of the Mayan Molars – Dentistry in the Ancient Mayan World." *Fresh Dental Care,* March 12, 2016. https://www.freshdentalcare.co.uk/post/the-mysteries-of-the-mayan-molars-dentistry-in-the-ancient-mayan-world.

"Plaster Leaf Cast Impressions." *Craft Project Ideas.* https://www.craftprojectideas.com/plaster-leaf-cast-impressions/.

Lloyd "Cyclone" Smith's Saddle

"Bonnie McCarroll." *Wikipedia.* https://en.wikipedia.org/wiki/Bonnie_McCarroll.

"How Much Weight Can Horses Comfortably Carry?" *Horse Lover's Math,* June 1, 2013. https://www.horseloversmath.com/how-much-weight-can-horses-comfortably-carry/.

"How to Tie a Lasso (Honda Knot)." *101 Knots.* https://www.101knots.com/how-to-tie-a-lasso-honda-knot.html.

Sale, Barry. "Casual Country: The Romance and Tragedy of Cyclone Smith." *Williams Lake Tribune,* June 30, 2016. https://www.wltribune.com/sports/casual-country-the-romance-and-tragedy-of-cyclone-smith/.

Williams Lake Bull

"Bull Stories a Part of Williams Lake's History." *Williams Lake Tribune,* April 18, 2014. https://www.wltribune.com/community/bull-stories-a-part-of-williams-lakes-history/.

ABOUT THE AUTHORS

S. Lesley Buxton is the author of the award-winning memoir, *One Strong Girl: Surviving the Unimaginable – A Mother's Memoir*. Her essays have appeared in *Hazlitt*, *Today's Parent*, *Still Standing*, *This Magazine*, and in the Caitlin Press anthology, *Love Me True*. An excerpt of *One Strong Girl* appeared in the March 2019 issue of *Reader's Digest* and has been translated into Spanish. For 18 years, she ran her own business, travelling around Ottawa and western Quebec teaching theatre and creative writing to children and teens. She has an MFA in creative nonfiction from the University of King's College in Halifax, Nova Scotia. To learn more about her, visit slesleybuxton.com.

Sue Harper is a retired secondary school teacher who has a BSc in psychology, an MA in English language and literature and an MFA in creative nonfiction. She has co-authored ten textbooks for the Ontario secondary English curriculum, and has written three books for reluctant readers as part of the series, *The Ten*, published by Scholastic. Her writing can also be found in magazines in Canada (*NUVO Magazine*, *Okanagan Life*), the United Kingdom (*France Magazine*) and New Zealand (*North and South Magazine*, *Forest and Bird*). In 2019, she published her memoir, *Winter in the City of Light: A Search for Self in Retirement*. She is the only person she knows who has explored all six hectares of Paris's Louvre Museum. To learn more, visit seniornomad.wordpress.com.

INDEX

For information on purchasing bulk quantities of this book, or to obtain media excerpts or invite the author to speak at an event, please visit rmbooks.com and select the "Contact" tab.

RMB | Rocky Mountain Books Ltd.
rmbooks.com
@rmbooks
facebook.com/rmbooks

Cataloguing data available from Library and Archives Canada
ISBN 9781771604178 (softcover)
ISBN 9781771604185 (electronic)

Design: RMB/Friction Creative

Printed and bound in China

We would like to also take this opportunity to acknowledge the traditional territories upon which we live and work. In Calgary, Alberta, we acknowledge the Niitsítapi (Blackfoot) and the people of the Treaty 7 region in Southern Alberta, which includes the Siksika, the Piikuni, the Kainai, the Tsuut'ina, and the Stoney Nakoda First Nations, including Chiniki, Bearpaw, and Wesley First Nations. The City of Calgary is also home to Métis Nation of Alberta, Region III. In Victoria, British Columbia, we acknowledge the traditional territories of the Lkwungen (Esquimalt and Songhees), Malahat, Pacheedaht, Scia'new, T'Sou-ke, and W̱SÁNEĆ (Pauquachin, Tsartlip, Tsawout, Tseycum) peoples.

We acknowledge the financial support of the Government of Canada through the Canada Book Fund and the Canada Council for the Arts, and of the province of British Columbia through the British Columbia Arts Council and the Book Publishing Tax Credit.